IMAGES OF WAR
THE GERMAN ARMY AT ARRAS

RARE PHOTOGRAPHS FROM WARTIME ARCHIVES

DAVID BILTON

Pen & Sword
MILITARY

First published in Great Britain in 2008 by
PEN & SWORD MILITARY
an imprint of
Pen & Sword Books Ltd,
47 Church Street, Barnsley,
South Yorkshire.
S70 2AS

ISBN 978-1-84415-768-6

A CIP catalogue record for this book is available
from the British Library

Printed and bound in Great Britain by CPI UK

Pen & Sword Books Ltd incorporates the imprints of
Pen & Sword Aviation, Pen & Sword Maritime,
Pen & Sword Military, Pen & Sword Select, Pen & Sword Military Classics,
Leo Cooper, Wharncliffe Local History

For a complete list of Pen & Sword titles please contact:
PEN & SWORD BOOKS LIMITED
47 Church Street, Barnsley, South Yorkshire, S70 2AS, England.
E-mail: enquiries@pen-and-sword.co.uk
Website: www.pen-and-sword.co.uk

Contents

Acknowledgements

A big thanks to my family for putting up with me writing yet another book – "Don't you have enough to do?" was the household cry – sorry! And again, what would I do without Anne Coulson to read the proof or the wonderful staff at the Prince Consort's Library who, so ably, assist me in my research? Thank you. As always it was a pleasure to work with the wonderful team at Pen and Sword.

Any errors of omission or commission are mine alone.

Introduction

It is not the purpose of this book to analyse in any detail the strategic, tactical, political or economic reasons for the fighting around Arras; it is merely to chronicle the events of 1914–1918 briefly in words, relying on the pictures to tell most of the story. It is not a chronological photographic record, more an attempt to provide a snapshot of the experiences of the German Army on the Arras Front during the four year period from October 1914 to October 1918. As the causes of the war have been dealt with at length in many books, I have only tried to set the scene for this book through the use of proclamations and statements from the Reich about the situation.

As with 'The German Army on the Western Front 1917-1918' the day-to-day chronology to show what was happening around Arras is taken from the German point of view. Although the area was strategically important, not every day is listed; for, as in every other area on the front, most days were no more significant than the last. If any day is missing, it is simply a case of: 'In the West nothing new'.

The area around the Arras front, from Lens in the north to Bapaume in the south, was an area of strategic importance to the Entente on account of the railroad centre at Arras, and on the German side the area was economically important because of its coal and agricultural output. It was also a relatively easily defended area as the French and, later, the British positions were on the lower ground. The German Army initially missed its chance here, and despite later efforts never succeeded in rectifying the mistake. In this book, the Arras Front covers the area from south of Lens to just below Bullecourt.

Fighting in the area can be divided neatly into five distinct phases. The first battle of Arras was fought during September and October 1914 when German troops occupied the town only to lose it to French counterattacks. Although German attacks were generally held, the French did eventually lose the strategic location of Vimy Ridge. The second battle of Arras comprised the French counter-attacks of 1915 – the Battle of Artois, fought between June and July designed to relieve pressure on the city. The fighting was severe and by 23 June the majority of the German trenches and dugouts before Arras had been captured. Early in July the French cleared the communications between Arras and Béthune and captured the nearby towns of Souchez and Neuville-St. Vaast. The third battle started when the British took over the Arras sector in March, but did not become an official battle until April 1917. After considerable mining activity, a decisive battle was fought between April and May of that year which resulted in the capture of Vimy Ridge and other important positions around Arras (for this battle I have used much material from *The German Army on the Western Front 1917-1918*). The fourth battle of Arras, during the German offensive of 1918, was short-lived and achieved little for the attackers. The fifth and final battle was fought during August and September 1918 when Allied forces attacked German positions to the east of Arras.

In each phase the fighting was hard and the casualties high; indeed those of 1917 rank among the highest of the war on the Western Front. It was not until the last battles though that the battle-front actually moved very far.

The town of Arras, like Ypres, was always just on the front line and earned the name of 'La ville martyre' with many of its public buildings destroyed by artillery and aerial attack. Below the city are the Boves, underground chambers that were used to shelter Allied soldiers and, after the war, to temporarily house civilians returning to rebuild their shattered town. During the war further tunnels were dug by British troops for the invisible movement of troops to the front line.

Throughout the book, German units are identified by italics and British and French troops by standard lettering.

A tree in the park at Boisleux-au-mont, south of Arras, showing the effect of blast from a shell explosion.

An artist's view of the northern sector of the Arras front showing the Douai plain from the heights of Arras.

Chapter One

1914

In Vienna, the local paper, the Weiner Zeitung, reported that 'In the night of July 25, it was made known that the Emperor of Austria had ordered a partial mobilisation of the Army and a partial calling up of the Landsturm.' Six days later, the *Reichsanzeiger* printed Imperial ordnance from Emperor Wilhelm, stating that 'the territory of the Empire, with the exception of the Kingdom of Bavaria, is hereby declared to be in the condition of war.' This was followed on 1 August by the order to mobilise from the Emperor: 'I order the German Army and the Imperial Navy to be placed on a war footing…August 2, 1914, is fixed as the first day of mobilisation.' Five days later, as a result of Germany being involved in a war that was forced upon the country, the Emperor called upon all Germans capable of bearing arms to defend the Fatherland.

While Austria and Germany prepared and mobilised, so too did the armies of France, Russia, Belgium and Britain. On 2 August, the French accused the Germans of crossing the frontier at three different points, shooting at the border personnel, stealing horses and killing a soldier. The next day, the German Ambassador in France, in his farewell letter, accused the French of violating Belgian territory and dropping bombs on Germany, giving his reason for leaving as the state of war that now existed between France and Germany. The die was cast – Europe would go to war.

As Britain entered the war, the Kaiser told the Reichstag 'I no longer recognise parties, only Germans'.

Ich kenne keine Parteien mehr, Kenne nur noch Deutsche.

Wilhelm II.

4. August 1914

Artist's impression of the use of cavalry during the Marne battle.

Generaloberst von Kluck, commander of I Army, who allowed his troops to deviate from the Schlieffen plan, giving the Allied troops a chance to counterattack.

French positions in early 1914 being held by troops, national guards and armed civilians – franc-tireurs; these latter men would be shot if captured as they were not considered to be soldiers by the German Army.

An artist's impression of a cavalry charge against well dug-in troops in the Vimy area.

A few days later, the German government informed the Belgian government that, although it regretted having to cross the frontier, this action was necessary because the French were already in Belgium trying to enter Germany in disguise. The French government were also warned about the use of civilians to fight the war: 'from information received from German troops it has become known that a war of the civil population has been organised in France, contrary to international law. In numerous instances, the civil population, under the protection of civilian clothing, have treacherously fired on German soldiers'. The warning continued, stating that, as a result, anyone not in uniform who takes part in activities that are detrimental to the German forces 'will be treated as a franc-tireur and instantly shot under martial law.' Civilian involvement was to affect the initial attack on Arras.

On 1 August, just before 1900 hours, the time set for *16 Division* to move into Luxembourg, the Kaiser countermanded the order, but by then a company of *69 Infantry Regiment,* commanded by Lt. Feldmann, had already crossed the border and taken their objective; the following day *Fourth Army* occupied the country. Next day, the Belgian government refused the German army entry and, from that point on, considered itself to be at war with Germany. On 4 August German forces crossed the frontier, meeting little opposition.

The commanding heights of Lorettohöhe were bitterly contested because of the excellent field of view they gave of Arras. Here the French attack against well dug-in troops.

While the German armies fought their way through Belgium, the French launched their own attacks in Lorraine, the Ardennes and on the Sambre. No matter how valiantly the French and Belgians fought, the German army kept moving forward. On 24 August, 'one million Germans invaded France. For the French and British the great retreat had begun. It lasted for thirteen days, blazing summer days' in which the German Army made a bid for a swift decisive victory. 'They were desperate days for the Allies whose only offensive plan had not survived the opening battles of the war', while the German troops were following the highly detailed Schlieffen plan.

Five of the seven armies 'scythed down towards Paris on a 75-mile front. For the troops on both sides they were days of endless marching under a scorching sun.' Even though the Allied troops were under constant pressure, their retreat was ordered and controlled, but each new action moved them closer to Paris – so close that, on 2 September, the French government left for Bordeaux.

However, a captured map showed that von Kluck's *First Army* was now headed for the gap between the French Fifth and Sixth armies and not for Paris. This exposed his army's right flank to attack; this deviation from the Schlieffen Plan when his troops were seriously over-extended, badly exhausted and exposed, both on their flanks and the rear, resulted in a general withdrawal from the Marne to the Aisne.

Cheering reservists are taken around Berlin in August; scenes like this were common across Europe at the start of the war.

A view of Arras after the bombardment of 6, 7 & 8 October, showing the damage to St. Géry Street.

14 *LA GRANDE GUERRE.* — *Arras.* — *Place de la Gare, Toutes les jolies maisons modernes de cette façade sont détruites.* — *Place of the Railway Station.* — *All those fine houses are destroyed.*

Arras railway station after the October bombardment.

Although Arras was in the path of the planned invasion route, the actual invading forces passed by, miles to the east, with the closest fighting being in the Somme region to the south. With the Allied attacks failing to push the Germans back on the Aisne, attention on both sides was becoming increasingly concentrated on the open flank to the west, and, 'by the time the battle on the Aisne was dying down, activity at the western end of the line was developing fast.' Arras would soon be part of the battle lines.

The end of the fighting on the Aisne brought about the final campaign of movement on the Western Front at the beginning of the war. Each side tried to outflank the other to the north: from the Aisne to the Somme through the Douai Plain and beyond. And as both sides raced towards the north, the various units involved leap-frogged past each other, taxing their lines of communication to the utmost in their efforts to move large bodies of troops to the north faster than the enemy could – but each manoeuvre ended in deadlock and trench lines.

The first German troops to enter Arras were a cavalry unit. After a three-day occupation, which included some looting and the requisitioning of goods and money, they were evicted by French light cavalry on 9 September. However, both sides were fighting in the Somme area and little further fighting took place. As the French forces were not available in sufficient numbers, the German Army was able to dig-in, in some cases only four kilometres away, and beleaguer the city. The period that followed and lasted for over thirty months was known as the 'Martyrdom of Arras'.

'While Falkenhayn's attention was being pulled away from his right to his centre and left, Joffre's purpose remained fixed. On the 25th itself he shifted XI Corps from the 9th Army to Amiens: by 1 October, using roads as well as rail, two more corps, plus three infantry and two cavalry divisions, had set off for Amiens, Arras, Lens, and Lille. Castelnau's army now embraced eight corps and extended along a 100-kilometre front. Its task was no longer to outflank but to hold, while a detachment under Maud'huy was drawn to the untenanted north-east, to Vimy and the Scarpe valley', while the southern sector was held by territorials.

On 26 September, after heavy fighting, the French took up positions along a line from Lassigny to Bray and 'the German *Cavalry Corps* moved further north to clear the front for the *II Bavarian Corps*' on the right of *I Bavarian Corps*. The next day the *Cavalry Corps* under von der Marwitz 'continued its way northwards, driving away d'Amande's French Territorials…and clearing the front for the *XIV Reserve Corps*' that moved on Albert. The offensive continued to make progress, but the French cavalry held von der Marwitz's troops just as the French Tenth Army was starting to detrain around Arras.

Arras Town Hall after the bombardment of October 6.

GUERRE 1914-15   ARRAS — Hôtel-de-Ville   après le bombardement du 6 octobre 1914
     WAR 1914-15   Town Hall after   the bombardment of October 6th 1914

Arras cathedral after the bombardment.

General Maud'huy, commander of the French Tenth Army at Arras, faced a strong German force, but was only given the four divisions of the French Cavalry Corps to the southeast of Arras and two reserve divisions at Arras and Lens. The plan was to begin an offensive from Arras-Lens southeast, against what was assumed to be a weak flank held only by cavalry. However, behind the cavalry, three corps had arrived ready to begin their own offensive. Now the French Tenth Army, scattered over a wide front, were in danger of being enveloped.

'Falkenhayn too continued to manoeuvre on his right wing. But although he pushed all his disposable forces towards Rupprecht, and on 28 September directed the *6th Army* to attack Arras, he did not forsake the possibility of a breakthrough in the centre'. Rupprecht hoped to hold Maud'huy 'frontally at Arras and, wheeling north round the city, to envelop the French left wing. To do this, on 3 October he reinforced the reserve corps operating north of Arras, and sent *IV Cavalry Corps* from Valenciennes, north of Lens, towards Lille'.

The Arras offensive was part of a three-pronged attack with the newly reinforced cavalry sweeping across Flanders to the coast. Antwerp was captured before it could be reinforced, and there was a strong offensive near Arras. The latter attack was launched on 1 October on the front Arras-Douai, by the *Guards, IV & I Bavarian Reserve Corps*, against Territorial troops of the French Tenth Army who were still preparing for their own offensive against the German positions.

On the morning of 2 October, General von Arnim's *IV Corps* was approaching the French lines from the direction of Cambrai and had a clear line of attack into Arras, except for troops commanded by the French General Barbot. These were dug into the small plateau of Feuchy to the northwest of Arras and were virtually isolated after other French attacks near Monchy failed, and the newly arrived French X Corps had run into the new German lines.

The next two days brought further success as the French were pushed out of

Lens and fell back to the southern outskirts of Arras. Village by village, the Bavarians beat back the French troops.

Any advance was met with stiff resistance. *9 Cavalry Division* fighting around Billy Montigny and Froquières, on 3 October, reported 'hours of bitter street fighting…in the struggle to drive the Morroccan (sic) troops and armed miners from their defences in houses and numerous mine-shafts.' The story was the same the next day in all of the coal mining districts to the northeast of Arras when the *Cavalry Corps* attacked as ordered. However, the terrain was not suitable for mounted warfare and the men fought a dismounted action against Moroccan troops and armed miners: 'step by step, the Jaegers and Cavalry troopers fought their way with carbines for possession of the locality, against an enemy defending from houses and pits; lacking bayonets, no headway could be made against massive factory walls without employment of heavier ammunition.' Once again, the spectre of the franc-tireur had risen.

The front of Arras Town Hall shortly after the three-day bombardment.

However, by the evening of 4 October, Arras was threatened with encirclement. The situation was desperate: General Maud'huy started to issue orders to abandon Arras, but Foch, his commander, had been tasked with stopping the retreat. Resistance stiffened, holding the German troops. Admiral von Müller, naval liaison officer at Army HQ in Charleville, recorded in his diary on 5 October that, when the Kaiser returned from the front, he was under the impression that a great victory had been won against the extreme left flank at Arras, but, as more news came in, he realised that this was not the case.

On 6 October, while *I Bavarian Reserve Corps* made progress on Vimy Ridge, to the south the advance of the *Guard* and *IV Corps* was checked. Near Liévin, just north of the victorious Bavarians, the day started quietly near pit 16. 'Few Frenchmen appeared in front, as the enemy utilised every possible cover for their movements, in a clever and careful manner. Now and then the French artillery sent its iron greeting into the towering structures of the pit.' Shortly after lunch the war re-

As the French troops pulled back, they destroyed bridges that might be useful to their enemy. Here cavalry pose on the remains of a railway bridge near Arras.

In the short time the two enemies fought each other in the streets of Arras, no quarter was given.

commenced as in 'all directions lines of skirmishers plunged forward, working their way along in rapid intervals; and simultaneously, a terrible cannonade assailed the pit…such as we had never experienced before. To crackling shrapnel and the explosion of high-power shells were added the din and uproar of shattered iron and glass and the falling of masonry. There were many killed and wounded in our midst…but the wide-reaching attack succeeded in gaining several trenches.'

A positional change allowed the defenders to take the French assailants in the flank and, in total disregard of the heavy losses, the first waves swept on, but 'then the counter-thrust followed, which resulted in a flight with coat-tails flying.' Firing upon the French with the shortest fuse setting possible till the ammunition gave out, and using every able-bodied man available to carry shells, the French advance was checked and held.

This near approach to the city resulted in the inhabitants being evacuated during an artillery barrage that lasted for three days. In the evening of 3 October an announcement was made that all men between eighteen and forty-eight had to leave Arras. Shortly afterwards women and children packed their essential belongings and left.

On 6 October, after receiving reinforcements, the French occupied the whole town after atrocious street fighting. During the day artillery bombarded the city and by 9 October over 1000 shells had hit the town. The central quarter of the city received the greatest attention; many of the city's finest buildings were destroyed. Afterwards, the bombardments slackened but nevertheless each day the city was shelled; it contained barracks and an important railway centre.

Hope now 'rested on the three Cavalry Corps, *I, II* and *IV* under von der Marwitz, outflanking the French line' and forcing them to withdraw. However, 'the attack gained no positive conclusion' and, by the evening of 6 October, both *I* and *II Cavalry Corps* had retired behind the Lorette Heights which they held, with difficulty, the next day, against vigorous French attacks. By the evening of 6 October 'the front had become stabilised near the line Thiepval-Gommecourt-Blaireville-eastern outskirts of Arras-Bailleul-Vimy-Souchez, on which the belligerents were to face each other' for many months.

However, the arrival the next day of the *XIV Corps* allowed the cavalry to pull out for an attack further north. After three further days of heavy fighting, the French retook Carency.

In Arras, the French prepared for the next attack while the Germans waited for their heavy artillery. On the afternoon of 20 October the storm broke: 21 and 28cm shells crashed into the city and by the following day the town centre was in ruins. Two days later, General Barbot's troops halted the attack on the eastern suburb of St. Laurent and then counterattacked, successfully halting the advance.

Positional warfare now took over from a war of movement. Both sides dug in. The

From the heights of Lorettohöhe, Arras was an easy target for heavy artillery.

French held the lower ground around Arras, constantly overlooked by the German positions on the ridges that surround the city. Infantry attacks continued on a greater or lesser scale with the artillery continually shelling Arras and the front lines. It was a busy part of the front where the wounded kept coming, as evidenced by a Swede touring the battle area: 'we took the great road to Arras, which we kept to as long as we possibly could without exposing ourselves to shellfire…at Boiry, almost levelled to the ground by fire and shell, we once more got on to the right track. Here the Red Cross flag was hanging from many houses, and we saw the wounded being carried into the hospitals. A column of light field howitzers rolled away towards Arras'. At the same time, life continued for those who had stayed behind. 'In a field some soldiers were placidly digging potatoes, and, near by, old men, women and children were gathering the sugar-beet.'

The authorities provided the troops with daily news sheets that were pinned on street hoardings to provide war news from all the fronts. As each daily edition was pinned up, troops eagerly read news about the situation in Russia, in the Argonne or closer to home on the Arras front. The *Bapaumer Zeitung* of 27 October provides a typical day's news. 'The fighting on the Yser-Ypres Canal front is exceedingly violent. In the north we have succeeded in crossing the canal with a strong force. East of Ypres and south-west of Lille our troops have advanced slowly after severe fighting. Ostend was yesterday bombarded by the English ships. In the Argonne our troops have likewise made progress. Several machine guns have been captured. We have taken a number of prisoners and two French aeroplanes have been brought down. West of Augustovo the Russians have renewed their attacks which have all been repulsed. At Ivangorad 1800 Russians have been taken prisoner. South-east of Przemysl the Austrians have scored several successes. Nearer to home east and north-east of Arras the enemy has received reinforcements. Nevertheless our troops have succeeded in making progress at several points. About five hundred British, including a Colonel and twenty-eight other officers, have been taken prisoner.'

Andreas Knopf, a typical early war soldier, posing ready for the front with full equipment, economy felt helmet and the floral decoration often given to departing soldiers.

A souvenir postcard for the troops to send home sending greetings from Roubaix, Lille and Arras; the first two towns were captured in 1914 as was Arras, but only for a matter of hours.

Zum frommen Andenken
im Gebete
an den tugendsamen Jüngling

Johann Grill,

Unterbutter-Sohn, Pfarrei Inzell,
Infanterist im 1. Res.-Inf. Regt.,
12. Kompagnie,
welcher am 4. Oktober 1914 bei Arras
in Nordfrankreich im Alter von 25
Jahren den Heldentod fürs Vaterland starb.

Hast fürs Vaterland gestritten,
Hast den Heldentod erlitten;
Und als wahrer Tugendheld
Schau'st Du nun die bess're Welt.
Süßester Jesus, sei mir nicht Richter, sondern
Erlöser! (300 Tg. Ablaß).

Ehre dem Andenken

des Herrn

Franz Stempfl

Unteroffizier
im Kgl. Bayer. 1. Reserve-
Infanterie-Regiment

gefallen am 6. Oktober 1914
bei Arras, Nordfrankreich

„Mein Jesus, Barmherzigkeit!"

Johann Grill, 25 year-old reservist of *I Reserve Infantry Regiment* who was killed in action near Arras on 4 October 1914.

Unteroffizier Franz Stempfl of *I Bavarian Reserve Infantry Regiment* was killed in action near Arras on 6 October 1914.

A view of Arras in late 1914 taken from the nearby hills.

ach dem Gefecht. Sanitäter geben einem schwerverwundeten Soldaten Wein.

After the fight, medics give a heavily wounded soldier a drink of wine to ease the pain.

Originalaufnahme vom Kriegsschauplatz.
Feldlager nach anstrengendem Marsche.

As the war situation was still fluid during the early months of the war, troops bivouacked on the march wherever was convenient.

Relationships between enemies were not always strained, especially among the young who quickly adapted to the change and many learned the language.

Three French soldiers in a reserve trench somewhere on the Arras front.

Air observation provided clues to the intention of the enemy. Here a soldier guards a camouflaged wagon.

Châteaux that were not damaged in the fighting were either turned into officers' quarters or field hospitals; this one became a hospital.

Aerial view of the French and German positions southeast of Arras at Tilloy near St. Laurent Blagny.

A divisional column parked up in a village behind the lines before unloading its supplies.

In Bereitschaft

A posed view of the front line, probably taken in a reserve position; exposure like this, in a front line trench, was extremely dangerous as both sides used snipers from the beginning.

ssengrab bei Thélus, Nordfrankreich.

Troops were buried were they fell, either singly or in mass graves – a mass grave in Thélus, to the east of Arras, taken in 1914.

As the younger troops moved on to new positions, older troops followed to set up garrisons.

To press his troops on to ever greater efforts, the Kaiser often visited the front areas. Here, on 4 October, he is seen leaving the headquarters of *IV Corps* commanded by General Sixt von Armin.

A postcard from the Bavarian War Ministry informing the parents of Infantry reservist Flügel of his death.

A view of no man's land after a French attack from the trees on the right – dead are strewn across the ground. Many of these would lie there for months or later be buried in shallow graves.

As the trench lines developed, soldiers settled into a more fixed way of life. Here cobblers mend war-weary boots at the battalion headquarters.

Kompagnie-Schuster im Unterstand

All sites considered of some value had to be guarded, no matter what the weather or how isolated.

Well behind the lines barracks were set up where troops could rest and train for further service in the trenches.

After the battle had moved on, each village had to be cleared of the rubble caused by the fighting. The work would be done by civilians where available, but often by low grade garrison troops, as in this picture.

To accommodate the large number of troops, large buildings had to be taken over as barracks, in this case the School of Arts, Industry and Commerce.

DOUAI (Nord). — L'École des Beaux-Arts, de l'Industrie et du Commerce transformée caserne par les Allemands. Visa Paris 2285. — The school of Arts, Industry and Commerce changed into soldiers barracks by the Germans.

Angres, at the foot of the Lorettohöhe, after the fighting had moved on.

Josef Unhoch, a professional hunter from Unterammergau, Landwehrmann was killed in the fighting near St. Laurent on 22 October 1914.

✠ **Josef Unhoch,** ✠

Zur frommen Erinnerung im Gebete
an den ehrengeachteten Herrn

Josef Unhoch,

Revierjäger in Unterammergau,
geboren am 6. Mai 1881, (Landwehrmann)
den Heldentod gestorben in Saint Laurent
bei Arras am 22. Oktober 1914.

Die Kugel, die Dich niederwarf,
Sie traf auch mich in's Herz;
Doch eines Helden Gattin darf
Nicht untergehn im Schmerz.
Die Kraft, die Dich im Kampf gestählt,
Sie sei mein Halt in Not;
Der Trost des Wiedersehens hält
Uns aufrecht bis zum Tod.

Druck von Josef Furst, Murnau.

A view of Vimy after the fighting was over; from a distance nothing had changed from before the war.

A photo of Vimy showing some of the damage caused by shelling, taken by J Ripper of the battalion staff of *I Bavarian Reserve Foot Artillery Regiment.*

The bombardment of Arras seen from Lorettohöhe.

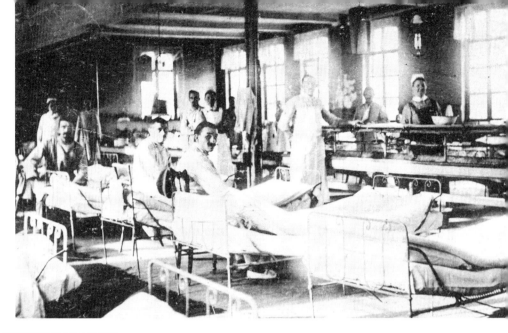

Heavy fighting on the Arras front produced heavy casualties needing care in temporary hospitals – here in a Lyceum in Doaui, well behind the lines.

Zum from-
men An-
denken im
Gebete

an den
ehren-
geachteten
Herrn

Heinrich Winkelhofer,

Schmiedsohn von Straß,
Pfarre Tundorf, Soldat im 1. bayr.
Res.-Inft.-Reg. 3. Bat. 11. Komp.,
welcher am 21. Dezember 1914 in der
Schlacht bei Arras im 30. Lebensjahre
den Heldentod fürs Vaterland starb.

Im heißen Kampf in Feindesla
Traf dich die Todeswunde.
Die Lieben dein im Heimatland
Traf schwer, die bitt're Kunde.
Den Heldentod fürs Vaterland
Bist Bester du gestorben
Hast mutig dir mit tapfrer Han
Den Himmelslohn erworben.

Mein Jesus Barmherzigke

Druck von Fritz Neerl, Laufen.

Heinrich Winkelhofer, thirty, a blacksmith's son, was killed in action on 21 December near Arras while serving with *1 Bavarian Reserve Infantry Regiment*.

A postcard sold to raise funds summed up 'The Big War 1914' in two pictures, the inundations of the Yser by the Belgians and the bombardment of Arras.

Chapter Two

1915

For the French army, 1915 was to be the worst year of the war for casualties: worse than Verdun and the Somme together. The total deaths for 1916 were 218,000, compared with 335,000 for 1915 during which the French attacked German positions in the Artois and in Champagne.

The French attacks during the year, coupled with British attacks further north, resulted in a new defensive system being dug with the first line close to Arras, the second line in front of Vimy ridge, running south through Athies, and a third line that ran south in front of Méricourt, Arleux, Oppy, Gavrelle and Fampoux. Later, a fourth defensive line was added – the Drocourt-Quéant switch.

The new year started as the old year had finished: both sides attacking and counter-attacking; positions being taken and re-taken or lost according to the whims of war; and, of course, the inevitable casualties. One German soldier recorded that it was not quite the New Year's Eve that they had hoped for when they found themselves in the forward trenches – full of water – as they waited to go out into no man's land. 'We crawled out of our positions to repair the barbed-wire entanglements and a patrol went out. Instead of the church bells of Berlin, the New Year was heralded by salvo after salvo from the French artillery, and quite a number of our chaps did not live to see the dawn of New Year's Day.'

Much of the early fighting was small scale, with limited objectives and of short duration, but it was still heavy on lives and was generally hand-to-hand with only one winner. The intensity of the fighting, the feelings it induced in him, and the changes it brought about in people, were recorded after the war by Private Westman: 'We got the order to storm a French position, strongly held by the enemy, and during the ensuing mêlée a French corporal suddenly stood before me, both our bayonets at the ready, he to kill me, I to kill him.

Like the Somme later, units that had fought on the Arras front were proud of it. A portrait of a Landwehrmann from *39 L.I.R*, a unit that had fought in the September battles around Arras in 1914 – Carency, Écurie, Neuville, Roclincourt and Souchez.

A 1915 view of Arras taken through a trench periscope.

Sabre duels in Freiburg had taught me to be quicker than he, and pushing his weapon aside, I stabbed him through the chest. He dropped his rifle and fell, and the blood shot out of his mouth. I stood over him for a few seconds and then I gave him the *coup de grace*. After we had taken the enemy position, I felt giddy, my knees shook, and I was actually sick.'

Such fighting claimed lives on both sides. After the battle, Westman's group of eight took stock of what had happened to them: 'two had been killed…a tram conductor…an office clerk…of the others (one) was a chimney sweep, two were farmers, one a student and another a teacher – all ordinary peace-loving people who a few months ago would not have harmed anyone. Now they told each other what they had achieved: one had killed a Frenchman with a pickaxe, another had strangled an officer, and a third had crushed the skull of a Poilu with his rifle butt. Now we were all murderers.'

Westman noted that soldiers quickly became inured to such violence. 'I saw a French soldier making ready to throw a hand grenade. I hit him so deeply between neck and shoulder with the sharp edge of a digging-tool that I had difficulty in extricating it. Soon afterwards I had to use it again. I no longer cared that my uniform was splashed all over with blood; I had become hardened.' But such experiences left their mark on the soldier. 'I saw the convulsions of my victim', wrote Westman, 'his face showing even in death the agonies I had inflicted on him, and his cramped hands held over the place where I had hit him. Long afterwards his glassy eyes stared at me in my dreams, and I woke up from my nightmare bathed in cold sweat.' Such experiences won some soldiers promotion; others were pushed into insanity.

However, by April, the French were in the ascendant and a major offensive was expected. After a month of preparation by artillery and mines on 9 May, after a violent artillery bombardment lasting several hours, the French Tenth Army attacked on a four mile front, with the centre advancing rapidly, leaving both wings behind. The very speed of the French advance was its undoing. 77 French division was one of the rapidly advancing units; it had successfully taken Hill 119, Givenchy and the outskirts of Souchez, when it came under such an intense bombardment that it was forced to retire as far back as Cabaret Rouge on the hill above Souchez. Such a rapid advance had not been planned for, and reinforcements were not available in time to stop German reinforcements arriving to halt the advance.

To the north, on 9 May, the British attacked after a short barrage. In response, two divisions were ordered to stand to arms but by evening it was clear that the danger had been averted and both divisions were moved south to reinforce *6 Army* between Lens and Arras opposite the French Tenth Army.

The aim of the French attack was to take Vimy Ridge: without this position the planned attack onto the plain of Lens and Douai would not succeed. This was the central part of the attack with subsidiary attacks against Bailleul on the right and Lorette on the left. The front attacked was held by only four divisions, but these were rapidly reinforced during the evening by two others, and, by 15 May, there were thirteen divisions opposite the French Tenth Army.

A captured French 12cm battery being inspected prior to being turned on its former owners.

The château at Monchy le Preux was used as a unit headquarters, here seen being guarded by a camera-shy guard. Printed on the wall are the ubiquitous road signs.

After a six day artillery preparation – the first real bombardment of the war - the French attacked with spirit and XXXIII Corps 'overran in one rush the German front defences and pressed on to a distance of 2½ miles on a frontage of four miles between La Targette and Carency. In less than two hours, the Arras-Souchez road was crossed and parties had pressed on to the crest of Vimy Ridge between La Folie farm and Souchez village'. As a result of this speed, there were no French reserves available, and within a few hours the advantages gained had been lost.

The battle reverted to the wearing-down process that was familiar from previous offensives. 'On the flat plain, behind the steep eastern slope of Vimy Ridge, the Germans unobserved could bring up reinforcements and supplies to their front defences, whereas the French communications lay across the broad open plateau in full view of the German observation posts.'

It was the overwhelming necessity for the French to take the positions that resulted in a high toll in life on both sides, but they were disadvantaged as explained by the *British Official History*: 'The fighting, mostly at close quarters in the trenches, was of a most desperate character. It developed into isolated encounters…with the stubborn German resistance, added to the natural advantages' of their positions making progress for the French very slow and expensive in terms of life, with many of the villages being taken house by house. Although the plateau of Lorette was occupied, the crest of Vimy Ridge was not reached; 'tactically the operation had ceased to offer any profit.'

To the French, the offensive 'led to the belief that a break-through on a scale far greater than that almost achieved at Neuve Chapelle two months previously was a feasible proposition, given an attack on a sufficiently wide front with adequate and methodical artillery preparation.' As a result, Foch decided to continue the attacks 'with the object of securing a good base for a further carefully prepared effort against Vimy Ridge.'

In the southern sector of the Arras Front was the Labyrinth, a fortified position that, from the air, appeared to be impregnable. The Labyrinth was a complex of trenches with barricades, trapdoors and deadly traps that cost thousands of lives to defend and eventually take. A contemporary Entente report described it as a unique stronghold. 'Inside it there is a complete and cunning maze, containing every species (sic) of death dealing device known to science, including numbers of gas and inflammable liquid engines. Underground tunnels, coupled with mines, compete with small fortresses containing guns' to destroy the attackers. It was a maze with a difference. 'In a maze one constantly turns corners to meet blank walls of hedge' but in the Labyrinth the corners were death traps, and 'from their subterranean refuge bodies of the enemy are liable to appear to the rear of the advancing attackers'. The Labyrinth was also linked to Neuville St. Vaast by underground tunnels.

A common method of movement across the flooded plains was the water ski or any piece of flat wood that was available and a paddle.

Musikkapelle
des kgl. bayr.
15. Inf. Rgts.
in Feindesland.

Troops out on rest needed entertaining and each regiment had its own band. Somewhere in enemy territory, resting soldiers of *15 Bavarian Infantry Regiment* had nice surroundings and a full band to keep them happy.

Having gained only a tenuous hold on a small part of the Labyrinth, on 15 May the French again attacked the position as well as Neuville St. Vaast and Souchez, but even after a two-hour artillery barrage and three separate infantry attacks, little progress had been made. Against such stiff resistance, the French called off their attacks, except for minor assaults against Neuville and the Labyrinth, until 16 June, when, after two days of little gain, the battle was brought to an end. The conditions in which the fighting took place were clearly described by a French officer who had fought there: 'The passages in which we were advancing were 18ft. deep, and often 24ft. or more. The water was sweating through in all directions and the sickly smell was intolerable. Imagine, too, that for three weeks we were not able to get rid of the dead bodies, amongst which we used to live night and day! One burrow, 120ft. long, took us thirteen days of ceaseless fighting to conquer entirely. The Germans had placed barricades, trapdoors and traps of all descriptions. When we stumbled we risked being impaled on bayonets treacherously hidden in holes lightly covered with earth. And all this went on in almost complete darkness. We had to use pocket electric lamps and advance with the utmost caution.'

By the end of the battle on 19 June, the French had made progress at Notre-Dame-de-Lorette, Ablain St. Nazaire, Souchez and Neuville St. Vaast, but the commanding heights were still in the hands of the occupier. Any territory surrendered to the French contained the remains of the previous fighting and was a constant reminder of the ferocity of the battle to hold the area. A French soldier noted that the trenches they had just taken were unpleasant; 'countless dead lay buried in the parapets of the trenches, dug in the thick of the battle during May. At every step, protruding through the wall, one saw here a hand or foot, there a tuft of hair or a piece of tunic.' The living inhabited the world of the dead.

Throughout the investment of Arras it was shelled, at times with great fury; 6000 shells, mostly incendiary, fell on 9 July, setting fire to the Cathedral and the Abbey of St. Vaast, while on other days it suffered only a few shots designed to keep the French on their toes. By the time the siege was lifted, 962 buildings had been completely destroyed, 1595 were destroyed beyond repair, and 1735 badly hit. Out of the 4521 houses in the city, only 292 were undamaged.

The situation returned to normal with minor attack and counterattack until the joint Anglo-French offensive of 25 September. This was a two-part offensive in the Champagne region and around Arras – the latter being the more important. It required the French to take Vimy Ridge and then attack from Arras across the plain of Douai, advancing between fifteen and twenty miles to cut the lines of communication and retreat.

A table diorama created during the 1930's to show the battle for Arras where the first drumfire barrage of the war occurred. It lasted for seventy hours.

The King of Bavaria was a regular visitor to wherever his troops were stationed; this is a parade in his honour on 6 February 1915.

A quiet moment in the trenches - whether fighting or not, everybody needed a haircut at some point.

'At 7:00a.m. on 22 September, the French opened their *Trommelfeuer* (drumfire – a barrage designed to weaken or destroy enemy positions) in the Champagne and in Artois.' This signalled the beginning of a 72 hour bombardment that in the end obliterated many positions, wiped out garrisons, swept away the wire, destroyed artillery observation posts and cut rearward communications. Extending far beyond the forward positions, the barrage was designed to hinder the movement of reinforcements to the front line. Despite the start of the French bombardment, Falkenhayn remained sceptical of French intentions; he did not believe that the French had the will to launch a major offensive, a belief that was reinforced by the easily repulsed French probing attacks on 24 September.

On 25 September, at 0915 hours, the French offensive began. In the southern sector of the attack, the French attacked at Vimy and Souchez while to the north the British attacked at Loos, on a six-mile front with six divisions supported by 114 heavy-calibre guns. The French force consisted of seventeen infantry divisions attacking on a twelve mile front with 420 heavy guns, 670 field guns and 260,000 rounds available, plus two cavalry divisions ready to press through any gap made in the German defences.

Joseph Wöss, a thirty-eight year old carpenter, of *I Bavarian Reserve Corps* who died after being shot in the lung near Gavrelle on 22 May 1915.

The attack moved forward rapidly and *6 Army* reported to OHL at 1230 hours that the enemy had broken into its position in a number of places and all its reserves were now involved in the fighting. Rupprecht requested immediate reinforcement.

The success of the French offensive was very limited and even the successful units made little progress against determined opposition. North of Arras, the French XXI Corps (13 and 43 Division) had Angres and the Bois de Givenchy as their ultimate objectives. Although initially successful, the French gains were lost to counterattacks during the night. Further south the situation was similar: either French progress was slow, or any positions taken were later lost. At Army HQ, Admiral Müller confided in his diary the seriousness of the situation: 'from the Champagne and Arras sectors disastrous news of successful (French) attacks against us and of heavy losses, including guns', this, coupled with news of the Greek Army mobilising, cast an air of depression over the officers working in the HQ.

Heavy artillery, because of the distance it could fire was generally well behind the lines; a gun troop pose with their mascot and two shells named 'baby Bertha' and 'Our darling'.

The next day, the stout defence held the French attack, and, by 10am, General Foch was told not to think of forcing Vimy Ridge because it would be useful to conserve troops for the Champagne offensive. French attacks continued and, although some territory was taken, the situation was very confused. The news that British attacks might falter resulted in further French attacks to the north of Arras - again with little French gain, but one loss was Souchez that fell to General Barbot's men. A soldier, Henri Barbusse, likened the state of the ground after the battle to a village that seemed to have disappeared. Another soldier described it more graphically as 'a trickling purée of wood, stone and bones ground and kneaded into the mud.' In his diary, Admiral Müller recorded a letter from Prince Eitel Friedrich (a son of the Kaiser) that reported the 'appalling losses of the *1st Guards Division* at Souchez (4,500 men)'. The next morning he left for the front to find out if the information was correct as it differed from the figures given by the General Staff. At Hénin-Liétard, near Arras, he conferred with two senior officers, Plettenburg and Schulenburg who were both 'very concerned by the bitterness of the fighting at Souchez' and the poor handling of the troops as they arrived to relieve *8 Corps*. As a result the losses, particularly of the missing, were terrifying.

However, French Tenth Army attacks on 28 September achieved an important success when part of its 6 Division reached Point 140, the highest point on Vimy Ridge in the German third line. 'Such alarm did this cause…that the greater part of the *Guard Corps*, which had been intended for use against the British, was diverted towards Vimy Ridge.' Even though the French gains were held during the night, General Foch and General Sir John French decided, during the morning of 29 September, that the offensive would be recommenced on 2 October; after much desperate fighting, progress was halted by reinforcements and much of the liberated territory returned to its previous occupiers. By 14 October the battle was over and the *Westheer* (West army) had proved its defensive strength and survived the initial assaults using only local reinforcements; divisions brought back from the Eastern front did not arrive until 5 October, by which time the attacks had been held. Casualties were heavy – 17,000 officers and 80,000 men against 150,000 French.

The Arras battles produced a mass of information that resulted in the eventual development of new defensive techniques. One clear message was that ' a well-constructed position, even one which has been subject to preparatory fire lasting for days, including the heaviest possible drum fire, can be held against repeated assaults, provided that the garrison remains absolutely calm and is led by energetic officers of iron will, who would prefer to die in the defensive line with their men rather than yield.'

With increasing troop numbers, at his first meeting with General Joffre on 23 December 1915, Sir Douglas Haig agreed to take over the twenty miles of front between First and Third Armies held by French troops; Arras was about to become part of the British front line. This would release French troops for use in other sectors – troops that would soon be needed at Verdun.

With food at a premium, many units were involved in crop production in one way or another.

As the shelling continued, Vimy suffered more and more damage, again recorded by keen photographer J Ripper.

On a good day, with no fighting, sniping, patrolling or shelling, life could be quite pleasant

Out on rest, soldiers could attempt to feel normal, especially when the canteen was well stocked.

Behind the lines regimental bands would play for passing troops and any villagers who had the time to listen.

Friedrich Kögel, of *3 Bavarian Reserve Infantry Regiment*, who had fought in the early campaigns, was killed at Roclincourt on 13 June 1915.

As the war progressed telephonic communication became more important – a soldier phones from the telephone bunker; open lines meant that the enemy could tap in to the conversation.

April 1915, an Aunt Sally type stall for troops out on rest in Willerval.

Another unit proud of its contribution to the Arras battle was the *Garde Jäger Battalion* that had fought there during the October campaign.

Movement in daylight brought down enemy artillery fire. Mail was essential in keeping up morale; here a post wagon of *2 Garde Reserve Division*, proudly displays some of the 100 shrapnel holes it received from an enemy shell.

Deutsche Feldpost 1914-15
Ein Feldpostwagen, der durch rund 100 Sprengstücke einer Granate beschädigt wurde

Carefully camouflaged field gun to disguise it from aerial reconnaissance and the following artillery barrages when the photographs were analysed.

Maibaum der Bayern in Farbus.

Zum frommen Andenken
an den tugendsamen Jüngling

Thomas Ostermaier

Ökonomenssohn von Frauenvils
Ersatz=Reserv. beim 1. bayr. Ref.=
Jäger=Batl. 3. Komp.

welcher am 12. August 1915 im
30. Lebensjahre bei Arras den Heldentod
für's Vaterland starb.

Thomas Ostermaier, who died aged thirty, on 12 August 1915 while serving with *1 Bavarian Reserve Jäger Battalion* near Arras.

A Bavarian Maypole erected in Farbus near Arras in 1915.

Vimy town square in July 1915 showing the gradual increase in damage to the town's buildings.

Two soldiers pay their respects to Lt Hebauer, who died on 2 October 1914 and was buried in the local church cemetery at Fresnes.

Aerial photograph of the trenches in the area known as the 'Labyrinth'.

The king of Bavaria awarding medals to soldiers who have distinguished themselves in battle.

Aerial photograph of the trenches in the vicinity of Douai in early 1915.

Reading and writing room for *2 Garde Reserve Division* and a tea room for *77 Reserve Infantry Regiment*, part of the division.

Lichtwirkung des die große franzöſ. Offensive vorbereitenden siebzigſtündigen Artillerie-Trommelfeuers u. der Leuchtgranaten, Ende September 1915.

An artist's impression of the night sky during the French autumn offensive in Artois at the end of September.

Zur frommen Erinnerung
im Gebete
an den tugendſamen Jüngling

Joseph Blöchl,

Bauersſohn von Langfeld,
Infanteriſt b. 10. Inf.-Reg.,
welcher im Kampfe bei Arras, den
Heldentod am 25. September 1915
im Alter von 26 Jahren erlitten hat.

Eltern trocknet Eure Tränen
Als mich traf das kalte Erz
War bei Euch mein letztes Sehnen
Brich nicht, brich nicht Elternherz.
Gönnet mir den Tod der Helden
Tragt als Helden Eueren Schmerz
Könnte man was ſchöneres melden
Brich nicht, brich nicht Elternherz.
Ihr Eltern und Geſchwiſter mein
Ich kehre nicht mehr zu Euch heim
Der letzt' Gedanke der letzte Blick
Eilte noch zu Euch zurück
Als ich ſtarb im Feindesland
Reichte niemand mir die Hand
Doch eh' mein Aug gebrochen
Sah ich den Himmel offen.

Süßeſtes Herz Jeſu ſei meine
    Liebe!   (300 Tage Ablaß.)
Süßeſtes Herz Mariä ſei meine
    Rettung!   (300 Tage Ablaß.)

Otto Morſak, Grafenau.

Joseph Blöchl, the son of a farmer in Langfeld, died on 25 September 1915 fighting with *10 Bavarian Infantry Regiment* near Arras.

June 1915 – an aerial view of the trenches near the Labyrinth complex, a hotly contested area.

Zur frommen Erinnerung im Gebete
an den tapferen Krieger, Jüngling

Josef Stampfl

Gütlers-Sohn von Dellenhausen,
beim 1. bayer. Infanterie-Regiment,

Inhaber des „Eisernen Kreuzes."

Gestorben für König und Vaterland
am 12. Oktober 1915 im Feld-Lazarett
zu Avion an den Folgen schwerer
Verwundung im 24. Lebensjahre.

Ach unser Sohn der lebt nicht mehr,
Er fiel auf dem Feld der Ehr'.
Er reicht uns nicht mehr seine Hand,
Die Feindeskugel zerriß das schöne Band.
Bitter, ach, ist unser Schmerz,
Doch unser Aug' schaut himmelwärts.
Wo Du weilst in ewiger Wonne,
Geschmückt mit einer Heldenkrone:
Denn, die für Herd u. Heimat sterben,
Vom Herrn als Lohn die Krone erben.

A. Lang, Buchdruckerei, Au.

Josef Stampfl, the twenty-four year old regular soldier from Dellenhausen who was serving with *I Bavarian Infantry Regiment* when he died in a field hospital at Avion on 12 October 1915.

French POWs taken during the September offensive to clear Lorettohöhe and its environs.

Chriſtliches Gebets-Andenken

an den ehrengeachteten Herrn

Joseph Weinberger,

Oekonom und Biehhändler in Altenburg,

Soldat b. 3. Reſ.-Inf.-Reg., 7. Komp.,

welcher am 8. Dezember 1915 infolge ſchwerer Verwundung im Alter von 32 Jahren den Heldentod fürs Vaterland erlitten hat. Er ruht im Soldatenfriedhof Freßnes (Nordfrankreich).

Im fernen Land Dein tiefer Schlaf
Nahm uns das Heimkehrhoffen;
Die Kugel, die Dich tötlich traf,
Hat ſchwer auch uns getroffen.
Und gibt's kein Wiederſeh'n hienieden,
So doch gewiß im ew'gen Frieden.

Mein Jeſus, Barmherzigkeit!

Heiligſtes Herz Jeſu, erbarme dich der ſterbenden Krieger!   300 Tage Ablaß.

Vater unſer.   Ave Maria.

Druck von F. X. Graf, Bad Aibling.

Joſef Weinberger,
Oekonom und Viehhändler
in Altenburg.

Josef Weinberger, thirty-two year old economist from Altenburg, serving with *3 Reserve Infantry Regiment,* who died on 8 December from severe wounds and was buried in the military cemetery at Fresnes.

Three soldiers pose in a deep and secure front line trench armed with rifle and model 1915 grenade.

Chapter Three

1916

'As 1916 began, the German strategic situation was stable if not favourable. Through the course of 1915, the German armies had advanced deep into Russia and had seemingly crushed the Russian offensive capability. Serbia had been dealt an even heavier blow, as a combined German-Austro-Hungarian-Bulgarian force occupied the country and ejected the remnants of the Serb army from the continent. The destruction of Serbia opened rail communications with Turkey, thus helping to shore up this beleaguered ally. In Italy and on the Western Front, the Central Powers had warded off powerful Entente offensives and looked likely to be able to hold off any similar attacks for the foreseeable future.' However, Falkenhayn was no closer to achieving the goals set in November 1914.

Both Falkenhayn and Conrad, the two General Staff Chiefs, agreed that the war needed to be ended by 1917 before both nations reached the end of their resources. How could this be achieved? An offensive that would exhaust the French followed by a 'counter-offensive to mop up the French and British armies after they had been bled white by their own relief offensives.' After this the Entente should fall apart allowing a negotiated settlement. Thus the die was cast for Verdun and the Somme.

Ludwig III, King of Bavaria from 1913 to 1918 when the kingdom became a republic.

On 21 February, the great offensive against the French positions at Verdun began, but at the same time a diversionary attack was made by an infantry corps against the Bois de Givenchy, by which they regained possession of the knoll at the northern end of the Vimy Ridge from the French Tenth Army. The next day the French informed the British of the seriousness of the attack and requested the relief of the two flank corps of the four holding the Tenth Army front. Later, the French Commander-in-Chief asked that, of strategic necessity, the Tenth Army should be relieved at once. As an offensive against the Tenth Army front was considered unlikely, Haig decided to take over the whole of the front.

Between 2 and 14 March the relief of the Tenth Army was completed, but not in

General Otto von Below (marked with X), seen here on the eastern front when he commanded *8 Army,* was the commander of *6 Army* during the British attacks near Arras.

the secrecy that had been intended. The British 46 Division went into the line on 9 March with advance parties going into the trenches wearing French helmets to disguise their arrival from enemy observation. However, the changeover was already known by 7 March. On that day a 'French listening post reported that a German patrol had looked in and were heard to comment that the British had not yet arrived.'

Whilst the British were moving in, OHL was anticipating its counter-attack response to the Entente relief counter-attacks; one favoured area was Arras but *6 Army* rejected this unless they were given more than the eight divisions promised. Falkenhayn rejected the proposal of a large-scale breakthrough attempt because there were insufficient troops available without a serious weakening of the other fronts.

6 Army were not deterred and proposed, on 16 March, an offensive that would result in the capture of Arras. The reasoning behind the proposal was sound: the British had only just taken over the sector, did not know their positions well and had very few reserves; taking the city would have a great negative psychological impact on the Entente. To take Arras, *6 Army* wanted to launch a two-pronged attack to the north and south, in two parts due to a shortage of artillery. The first attack would take the heights at Ecurie and, after the heavy artillery had been moved, the southern attack would be launched.

The Entente powers were in no position to launch a relief attack anywhere on the front and Verdun was using up the OHL reserve more quickly than anticipated; there would be no major second offensive, only a secondary one. Falkenhayn telegraphed *6 Army* on 4 April and asked whether they would be prepared to launch their offensive with four additional divisions and an increased number of heavy artillery batteries. Their reply was immediate: four divisions would allow them to take Loos and it would need three weeks of preparation before the attack. On 10 April, Falkenhayn ordered them to continue preparations for the Arras attack.

The rapid rebuilding of the poorly constructed French trenches by their new inhabitants made any attack more difficult. As a result, *6 Army* requested eight extra divisions and more heavy artillery for the two-stage attack. Again events at Verdun caused a change of plans and the attack was put on hold.

After Flanders, the area was dry and bright. The relieving British troops found that the area from the Somme to Arras had seen practically no fighting since the line had settled

Franz Matzinger, twenty-three, a farmer's son, who died on 23 January 1916, from a head wound caused by shell splinter, while serving in *15 Bavarian Infantry Regiment*.

down in 1914. 'North of this in the Vimy sector, where the French had recently lost

A timber dump at Feuchy, with construction materials for use in the trenches.

Easter 1916 at Angres, resting medics pose for the camera.

ground in the German attacks of the 8th and 21st February, the line was found to be in a bad condition: the trenches were poor, without wire and without dugouts.'

The change from French to British occupancy on the Arras Front was noted by one soldier: 'Early in March 1916 the British took over the sector from Arras south to the Somme Valley. The Germans were alerted to the presence of these newcomers by the white puffs of their high-bursting shrapnel, the British and American stampings on the munitions, and the unwelcome increase in the numbers of the enemy machine guns. The leisurely tic-tac of the French machineguns, which ceased after every twenty-five rounds to allow a strip to be inserted, was replaced by the headlong and endless chatter of the new weapons, which sprayed the landscape with bullets and endangered our approach routes by night.'

This was the opposite of what had been the norm in the area. While the French had lived in trenches without wire, the German positions were protected by thick wire belts. There was little firing, with both sides living by a policy of 'live and let live'.

Du schiedst von uns mit tränenfeuchtem Blick,
Und kehrst nimmermehr in's Vaterhaus zurück.
Als Held hast Du gekämpft mit Herz und Hand
Für Gott, den Kaiser und das Vaterland.
D'rum ist nun Dein nach göttlichem Geheiss,
Die Himmelskrone als höchster Siegespreis.
O guter Sohn u. Bruder dort in des Himmelshöh'n,
Da möchten wir Dich einstens wiederseh'n!
D'rum bei Gott dem Herrn, im ew'gen Licht
Vergiss uns Trauernde im Erdentale nicht.

Süsses Herz Mariä
sei meine Rettung ! (300 Tg. Abl.)

Mein Jesus Barmherzigkeit.
(100 Tage Ablass.)

Barmherziger Jesus,
gib ihm die ewige Ruhe!

Zur frommen Erinnerung im Gebete

an den ehrengeachteten Jüngling

Michael Deisenberger,

Kaufmannssohn von Unterammergau,
Soldat b. kgl. bayr. 20. Jnf.-Reg. 8. Komp.,
geboren am 21. Juli 1895,
den Heldentod für's Vaterland gestorben
am 1. Februar 1916 bei Arras.

Buchdruckerei Oberammergau (H. Uhlschmid)

Michael Deisenberger, a twenty-year old businessman from Unterammergau, who died a hero's death on 1 February 1916 while serving with *20 Bavarian Infantry Regiment*.

Such an atmosphere encouraged verbal exchanges, when the trenches were close enough, and even led to the troops exposing themselves at will without fear of drawing hostile fire.

While the southern sector had been very quiet since 1914, the opposite was true of the northern part of the line, as evidenced in the sections on 1914 and 1915. Even though the German army had fought hard, the French had made some gains, but the strategically important Vimy Ridge defences had resisted all attempts at capture. Just before the British takeover of the sector, surprise German attacks were successful, and the French were pushed back on two occasions. On 8 February 'a length of trench half-a-mile wide, south of Central Avenue' was captured and on 21 February, 'the first day of the attack on Verdun, a knoll at the northern end of the ridge, opposite Souchez, known later as "The Pimple", the only place where the French had gained the crest of the ridge' was also lost, removing the only high point on the ridge held by Entente troops.

Vimy Ridge 'extends for nine miles from the valley of the river Scarpe, in front of Arras, to the valley of the Souchez stream, in which lie the villages of Souchez and

Crown Prince Rupprecht of Bavaria, overall commander of the Armies on the Arras front.

Georg Hopper of *12 Bavarian Infantry Regiment* who was killed on 17 July 1916.

Chriſtliches Andenken im Gebete
an den tugendſamen Jüngling
Georg Hopper,
Gütlersſohn von Riedersheim,
beim 12 bayr. Inf.=Regt., 2. Komp.
Geſtorben am 17. Juli 1916 im 21. Lebens=
jahre den Heldentod fürs Vaterland.

A farm in Wancourt – life continued around the shell holes.

Barbed wire entanglements in Beaurains, a suburb of Arras.

Carency, captured by the French in May 1915.' However, only the northern end is usually called Vimy Ridge. Beyond the Souchez valley, facing north, is the Lorette ridge and at the eastern end stands the chapel of Notre Dame de Lorette (this replaced the church destroyed during the fighting of 1914 and 1915, of which the only remnant when the British arrived was part of a brick wall).

'The western slope of Vimy Ridge is gentle, but cut into, just behind the British front line of 1916, by a branch of the Souchez valley running southwards, known as Zouave valley, which therefore narrows and accentuates the end of the ridge.' Zouave valley was named after the men who had fought there during the battles of 1915; many of them had not left and could be seen in the valley, 'unburied and unpleasantly close to the trenches'; they were rotting but still dressed in their scarlet pantaloons.

'The eastern slope drops sharply to the plain of Douai. Along almost the entire length of the ridge the Germans held the summit; only at its northern extremity did the line taken over by the British from the French lie near the top, and even there the crest was in No Man's Land, with the trenches of the two adversaries on the slopes on either side.'

The troops enjoyed perfect observation over the British forward area and

Military cemetery in the churchyard at Angres in the summer of 1916.

approaches, so that, for the Allied troops, positioning artillery was a particularly difficult problem. The maze of old and new trenches and gun positions deeply dug in the chalk gave the British troops some small security, simply because it was not possible to shell all the old positions; when they were shelled many were unoccupied; these latter were repaired and occasionally occupied in order to further confuse the German gunners.

On the other hand, the eastern slope of Vimy Ridge was so steep that the Germans were able to 'place trench mortars and supporting troops close to the front line entirely concealed from ground view and safe from all but very high angle fire. The plain beyond, though visible to British observers on the Lorette ridge, which afforded good distant observation, was covered with the numerous villages of the Lens coalfield, and therefore ideal for the concealment of guns.'

On paper, the front defences along Vimy Ridge consisted of three lines but, when taken over, were found to be of the crudest description, and entirely lacking in continuity. 'The trenches were described by the incoming troops as merely shell holes joined up; hastily organized positions in mine craters; a line of detached posts, accommodated in grouse butts; straight trenches without traverses. In places actually only a few sandbags laid on the ground marked the line. The section opposite the Pimple was reported as the worst.' Here, the newly arrived British troops found that the continuous trench that appeared on the map did not exist. The whole area was a quagmire, impossible to use as an attack point; it was difficult enough just to get to the trenches – only feasible at night and in the open - and even then only with great difficulty and in deep mud.

Conditions rapidly improved for the British as spring set in; the surface was soon bone dry except in Zouave Valley. Fortunately – for the German defenders – the British found few good communication trenches. Most were unfit for use, so the movement of materials for any future attacks against them was slowed down. Most of the communication trenches were undrained and insanitary. Around the area lay months-old dead bodies and the detritus of warfare. 'The wire, where any existed, was thin and weak, or in bad condition; the positions for machine guns were very poor. The dug-outs, except those some distance from the front, were small, damp and bad…the ground (was) sufficiently organized for the launching of an offensive, but offered only precarious tenure as a defensive line.' It was a state of affairs – new troops in a new area with poor defences – ready for a keen and watchful adversary to exploit.

While OHL was brewing its own plans, the British troops let them know that this was no longer a quiet area of the front by firing a few shells over their heads as a warning of what was to come. However, both sides realized that their defences were

Captured British aircraft near Arras on 29 March 1916.

The cemetery of an elite unit, *I Garde Reserve Regiment,* at Fresnes.

inadequate and hostilities ceased for a week while both sides dug, day and night, in full view of each other. When active hostilities were resumed, artillery fire, backed by excellent observation, prevented the British from completing their work. A fact noted by the Battalion History of 1st/4th Leicesters was that 'for sheer discomfort Vimy took a lot of beating', and after all the hard work restoring parapets and parados, and filling sandbags with sodden earth, the arrival of a minenwerfer could at once destroy ten yards or more of trench.

'Whilst the Germans had been smiling over the parapet, they had been pushing on below' recorded the *British Official History*. The British had taken over an active mining area in which the German Army had the upper hand, with many deep tunnels in place under the British lines. This, coupled with the poor defensive positions and the superior observation positions held by the German army, should have resulted in the British army pulling back to better positions, especially as this was not to be an offensive area of action. However, this would have appeared as an insult to the French, so Haig ordered the troops to take action, by mining and frequent raids, that would suggest a forthcoming Spring offensive.

British casualties were heavy for the next three months but slowly the German mining troops lost the initiative; four mines on 3 May and a further five on 15 May secured new observation positions for the British, giving greater visibility over

German positions. However, there was no retaliation or counter-attack by the German forces except heavy bombardment of the craters every night. This was a change from the norm; before, newly exploded craters had been hotly contested, with infantry rushing to capture the near lip of the crater, while the enemy who had not fired the mine, replied with artillery and both sides opened up with machine-guns. At such times, 'there was much bombing, but the rifle and the bayonet were rarely used.'

Further British casualties were caused by sniping. Again the upper hand was held by the Germans, whose snipers stayed in one area and identified the vulnerable positions, while the newly arrived British troops inevitably lacked knowledge of the terrain. These newly arrived troops were not well equipped for trench warfare and, to make up for the shortfall, resorted to handmade equipment, catapulting beer bottles filled with explosives, designed to explode two seconds after they had arrived in the opposing trench.

Under French occupancy the atmosphere in the area had mainly been one of 'live and let live' and initially this was continued by the British in some sectors; 18 London Regiment provided the troops opposite them with a copy of 'The Times' on one occasion. However, the transfer of the Saxon division and completion of tunnelling towards the British lines created a tension that was broken on 26 April with the exploding of a mine near the Pimple. Unfortunately for the attacking force, the British had anticipated such an action and their front line was only lightly occupied; even so they managed to secure and consolidate the near lip of the crater holding and stopping the attacking forces. Expecting a further mine, the British blew a defensive camouflet mine that prematurely detonated the mine and created a huge crater. Heavy casualties were inflicted on 6 London Regiment when a third mine was blown between the two previous mines, but again the British managed to restore their line and hold their positions.

In retaliation the British fired four mines on 3 May and under covering artillery fire rushed troops forward, successfully occupying the British side of the three craters formed – the fourth mine explosion did not break the surface – while Pioneers and Sappers constructed defensive positions on the British near lip. At dawn the British troops retired to the newly prepared positions.

Every effort had been taken to make sure that the British were unaware of the carefully planned offensive against them. The tactics were simple: the systematic obliteration of the British front line using trench mortars, destroying the British defences on the ridge. This was to be followed, for a few days before the attack, by the artillery registering on communication trenches and batteries in the attack sector. All this made the British infantry officers suspicious, but air reconnaissance provided no clues, and British Intelligence pointed to the German shortage of men

Camouflaged anti-aircraft guns near Roeux, east of Arras.

and artillery for such an attack. As a consequence, the transfer of five divisions from the British First, Second and Third Armies to strengthen the Fourth Army prior to the Somme offensive went ahead with all the necessary movement of Army, Corps and Divisional headquarters that this involved.

Fortunately for the attacking troops, the area for the forthcoming offensive was against British troops affected by the new boundary changes to the army and corps in the sector. The Berthonval sector was in a state of flux: signal traffic disturbance, no arrangements to ensure unit cohesion, no means of gathering intelligence and processing it. Not only had the sector been transferred to another army but to a different corps and a new division was taking its positions for the first time with only two battalions holding the front line. All of this was happening in a sector that was easily and clearly overlooked, with every British move easily registered.

The attacking troops had further advantages over the British defenders: the British front was held as an outpost line, with detached posts that could be approached only under cover of darkness, and thus had to be held by small numbers of troops for unrelieved twenty-four hour periods, starting at 2100 hours. Serious resistance would only be encountered much further down the slope; the ground was wet and any progress the British made in their defensive programme would be destroyed every night by artillery fire. As a result the attacking forces would face virtually no wire on the British front line, a support line that was only superficial, and troops in the detached posts who would have no shelter. All the odds were stacked in favour of the attackers.

Unusually, on both sides the commanding officers were experienced staff officers without combat experience; this was to be their first blooding. General von Freytag-Loringhoven was Generalquartiermeister (Deputy Chief of the General Staff) of the Supreme Command, under Falkenhayn, and, prior to that posting, had been senior liaison officer at the Austro-Hungarian Great Headquarters. He was anxious to have some experience at the front and in April was given a six weeks' leave of absence to replace General von Zieten, commanding officer of *17 Reserve Division*, who was sick. Shortly after, he was given command of *IX Reserve Corps* (General von Boehn was on leave due to poor health). Facing him was Lieutenant General Sir Henry Wilson who been sub-chief of the General Staff in France and also senior liaison at French Great Headquarters.

General Freytag-Lorighoven discovered that he had not taken over a quiet front. In his reminiscences he recorded that 'the casualties, which we suffered by mine explosions and continual night attacks, aroused in me lively anxiety…things could not go on as they were…If by attack we could throw back the British over the position we had held until the end of September 1915 [before the French attacks], and so rob them of all their mine shafts, and hold the position won, we should have tranquillity.' A plan was then conceived and approved by the Army Commander, and, thanks to his influence at headquarters, 'far more than the necessary heavy artillery and ammunition were allotted' in order to attain a successful operation.

If he had asked his men, they would have agreed that something needed to be done to stop the British mines. The history of *163 Regiment* explained their effect: 'These continual mine explosions in the end got on the nerves of the men. The posts in the front trenches and the garrisons of the dug-outs were always in danger of being buried alive. Even in the quietest night there was the dreadful feeling that in the next moment one might die a horrible and cruel death'. The men felt defenceless and powerless against them. This view was shared by *86 Regiment* which agreed that something must be done: 'Our companies had suffered heavy losses through the British mine explosions. It was accepted that other large parts of our trench system were undermined and might fly into the air at any moment'. The answer was an attack to gain possession of the mine shafts and bring an end to underground warfare for as long as possible.

For the attack on a divisional front of four miles, the infantry were to be supported by eighty batteries, of which forty were new. Situated between Liévin to the west of Lens 'and Vimy village, most of the guns were skilfully concealed amid houses and buildings. Very careful preparations were made. The British position was photographed from the air', and, in order to prevent British Intelligence getting wind of the operation, 'additional aeroplane squadrons and anti-aircraft guns, partly mounted in lorries, prevented British fliers from coming over and seeing any signs of the mounting of an attack.' As a result of these measures and strict telephone secrecy, there was an uninterrupted flow of heavy lorries carrying ammunition to the front areas.

The day and night of 20 May were comparatively quiet in the British trenches, apart from a considerable amount of trench mortar fire that caused anxiety at the divisional level but, the next morning, between 0500 and 1100 hours, the Berthonval sector and the sectors on either side were heavily shelled. After a lull of four hours, an intense bombardment began. It landed on the British front line, the observation posts, the communication trenches, the Zouave valley, and even beyond the battery positions to the British headquarters (four miles back) and the billeting areas, seven or eight miles from the front line.

'The whole front area was soon enveloped in a cloud of smoke and dust, so that the British artillery never really knew when the assault was delivered; and confusion was rendered worse by bursts of lachrymatory shell. All accounts agree that never had such a bombardment been seen, and spectators could only wonder that there was any rifle fire' from the British when the assault took place. In the four hour barrage 70,000 shells were fired that caused severe damage to both the infantry and the artillery. In retaliation, the heavy artillery of three British corps returned fire but with little effect.

At 2145 hours the barrage moved a further 150 yards into the British lines, a mine was fired under the British trenches at the head of Royal Avenue, and one minute later, the assault started. The smoke clouded the British defenders' vision and not until the attackers were half-way across no-man's-land could they be made out in the dust and smoke. By then it was too late; resistance along the British front was negligible, 'for the rifles and the bombs of the few dazed defenders still unwounded were unserviceable or buried', whilst their artillery was unable to assist them due to a shortage of ammunition and cut telephone lines. As the attacking troops came rushing through 'the front and support lines without pause in overwhelming numbers'; the British were unable to resist the onslaught. They were saved by the artillery of their enemy who ran into their own barrage due to the speed of their advance. Although there was little initial resistance, when the barrage moved on, sheltering troops emerged, and hand-to-hand combat took place.

The situation was desperate enough for the remaining British troops to man the reserve line, so desperate that the British had to bring up reserves in the form of

Whenever possible, military cemeteries were maintained neatly, using military and civilian labour.

three companies of Royal Engineers to fill the line. Unfortunately for the rest of the attackers, they did not advance as quickly or as far, capturing only small sections of the support line and the front line of the outposts. Although British resistance was stiff, it did not stop the important loss of all their mineshafts, except one at the head of Royal Avenue. Having achieved their target, the troops dug in and waited for the British counterattacks. These started almost immediately – some were successful, but others floundered against troops well dug in behind wire.

The next day, 22 May, was comparatively quiet and British planes located most of the batteries that had caused devastation the day before. Attempts to penetrate the British lines were stopped by British fighting patrols, so no information about the new British positions could be gained. No attempts were made by the British to recapture the lost ground, the only activity being their shelling of the lost territory while they prepared a counter-attack. In return British positions in Zouave Valley were heavily shelled after a British deserter revealed that a counter-attack would take place that evening.

At 2025 hours the British assault was launched after just over an hour's intensive bombardment. Its object was to recover the old support line and, if possible, the old front line to form a new support line half-way between it and the Talus des Zouaves. However, the British assembly area for the attack was heavily bombarded at 1130

A quiet moment in the trenches at Lorettohöhe during the summer of 1916.

hours with in an increase in the shelling at 1400 and 1800 hours. Just before 2000 hours, three separate barrages landed on the area containing the attacking troops. The desired effect was achieved. The British 99 Brigade attack was stillborn, except for one company who did not the receive the order to abort the attack. Having advanced through the machine gun fire that swept no-man's land, the company reached the front line. When attempts were made to bring it back, it was realised that it had been wiped out.

British battalions on the right and left flank of the attack also moved forward. The defenders fell back against the bombing onslaught but quickly counter-attacked and retook the positions, only to lose and regain them again in quick succession.

No further attacks were made by the British and the front quietened down. Two British reconnaissance flights the next day found that there was little activity behind the lines and from this surmised 'that the attack had been a local one with a limited objective'. However, the very large number of batteries brought up for the attack, the amount of ammunition used, together with the pushing forward of saps and the amount of mining, inclined the British Third Army Commander, General Allenby, to believe that this could be the prelude to a full scale attack on Arras via Roclincourt.

With so many troops committed in Russia and at Verdun, there was no real possibility of this success being built upon, and the British were left alone. What the operation at Vimy had demonstrated again to the British was 'that given sufficient artillery and observation, it was possible' to drive them 'out of any small portion of the line'. At 2450, the British casualty rate was nearly double that of the attacking force – 1350. The battle was described by one British General as 'the best executed trench raid carried out on the Western Front', and experienced British soldiers 'declared that the fire upon this occasion was among the most concentrated and deadly of the whole war.'

Even though the intentions of the Entente on the Somme were clearly known, *6 Army* was holding a shorter line than *2 Army* there, with seventeen and a half divisions and large amounts of heavy artillery. Falkenhayn intended to launch his counter-offensive at Arras after the British had exhausted themselves on the Somme. He assumed that the line at Arras would be held by second-rate and inexperienced divisions that would provide less resistance, allowing any local breakthrough to be turned into a strategic success. To ensure success, OHL kept some of its best divisions deployed near or with *6 Army*. With *2 Army* reinforced to take the Entente offensive and continued pressure on the French at Verdun, 'forces for the counter-stroke had been mustered' and their deployment begun.

However, the reserve divisions carefully kept back for the counter-offensive were needed elsewhere. The success of the Russian offensive took four of these divisions to the Eastern Front and by 9 July seven additional divisions had been sent from the reserve and *6 Army* to bolster *2 Army* on the Somme. 'As the summer wore on and the attacks on the Somme increased in their intensity…losses were so high that…Falkenhayn instituted a major reorganization of the *Westheer*'; as a result *6 Army* lost most of its best units to *2 Army*. By the end of August the reserves available to OHL consisted of just the *Guards Ersatz Division*. The Arras counter-offensive would never happen. On 29 August, Falkenhayn was replaced by Hindenburg and Ludendorff.

Troops in the trenches saw the Canadians taking over as their opponents on the Vimy Front during the autumn of 1916. Immediately, and to their chagrin, what had been a comparatively peaceful area became very active with trench raids and increased artillery fire. Such was the intensity of the fire at times that, in early December, the Canadians found an appeal on the barbed wire: 'Cut out your damned artillery. We, too, are from the Somme'.

While the rest of the year was relatively calm on the Arras Front, the battles at Verdun, in Russia and on the Somme impacted badly on manpower resources and on the ability to hold a continuous stretch of trench from the North Sea to Switzerland. General von Kohl wrote that 'the casualties suffered by Germany hit it harder than did those of the Allies' and each year it was more difficult to replace the losses. The commander of *27 Infantry Division* ably summed up the position of the German Army at the end of 1916: 'The formations which were deployed during the Battle of the Somme were very worn down physically and their nerves were badly affected. The huge gaps torn in the ranks could only be filled out by returning wounded, nineteen-year-olds who were too young, or by combing out from civilian occupations, men who, to a large extent, due to their physical condition or mental attitude, could not be regarded as fully effective troops'.

A withdrawal to the Siegfried Stellung would both reduce the length of the front line and remove a large salient; such a reduction would also increase the number of troops available as reserves. It was an obvious choice but *OHL* did not sanction the withdrawal.

The winter of 1916-1917 was wet and made work on the defences a never-ending task. In theory a regiment had a battalion in the line, a second battalion in reserve while the third was behind the line, out of artillery range at rest – a euphemism shared by their British counterparts for work, work and more work, often back in the front line; reserves had tasks to perform even in the severe wet: 'cement would not set, trenches flooded repeatedly, and the drainage table of the plain rose to the point where two-foot holes soon filled with muddy water.' To add to the problem, the Canadians facing Vimy ridge, 'had an irritating habit of shelling rear areas as well as forward trenches; all available man-power was needed to keep open the lines of communication.' General von Bachmeister felt that, with the severe bombardment of rear areas and the 'systematic destruction of artillery positions, dug-outs, rearward communications and the front line', the British had a plan. 'One result, quite aside from the damage caused, was that the soldiers on the ridge and in the rear were overworked and inadequately rested.'

Many of the troops in the Arras sector came from Bavaria and were used to a high meat content in their diet. As well as all their other problems the rations were bad and even the food for the forward trenches – already of poor quality- was also noticeably meagre as regards meat. 'Out of the line, in reserve, it was even worse: there were meatless days, which made the mining villages that served as billets seem colder and damper than they already were.' The troops were hungry as well as tired.

Out of the line, although their rations were inadequate, the Bavarian troops still managed to stay happy by singing. And in many cases their life was better than the life of a civilian back at home, but this was small comfort which gave no pleasure knowing that their families, especially the children, were faring worse than they were. But of course, as in every army, the officers were better off than their men: they had freedom of movement and could travel further, back to towns like Valenciennes where they could enjoy, temporarily, a life of café society and security.

To add to their problems, the war news generally contained little to be cheerful

1916

H. Vogel. 16.

Wir streiten und
Wir leiden gern,
Zeigt uns dieß Bild
Der Weihnacht Stern.
Die von der 6ten Armee

6 Army Christmas card produced by *6 Army* field Printing section as a field postcard to send home.

about, and the news from home was gloomy. Goods were in short supply and in some areas food staples were rationed. Wives missed their husbands and complained about the shortages: 'How long is the war going to last before you are all destroyed?…things are very bad for us. There is neither beer, gin, petroleum, soap, benzine, sugar, coffee nor meat.'

The life was dangerous, and nearly always wet. Their uniforms smelt of sour sweat, and the trenches in which they lived, though deeper and better built than the ones occupied by 'die Engländer', were foul with years of occupation. Nevertheless, although it took time and determination to maintain an appearance of smart professionalism, it was done. By stand-to each morning, boots were clean, greatcoats brushed, faces shaved and refuse buried. Their officers demanded it.' And according to the reports of men captured by the Canadians, officers were another problem in the lives of the men holding the ridge.

But life was not all bad on the ridge. On Christmas Day, two men of Princess Patricia's Canadian Light infantry arranged a truce with their opponents. The two sides met in no man's land and exchanged cigars and cigarettes and attempted to communicate. The peace was short-lived; at 2200 hours the Canadian troops in the neighbouring battalion raided their opponents' trenches and stole all their Christmas presents, thus smartly ending the truce.

Chapter Four

1917

At the end of 1916 the Siegfried Stellung was only to be regarded as a 'factor of safety' and there was no intention of voluntarily retiring to it; however, by the middle of January, General von Kuhl summed up the situation at the principal General Staff officers' conference: 'We can no longer reckon on the old troops; there is no doubt but that in the past summer and autumn our troops have been fearfully harried and wasted'.

British Fifth Army winter operations made the situation even worse and, by the end of January, it was acknowledged that the positions presently held by the German Army on the Somme 'were bad, the troops worn out', and that they were probably not in a condition to stand such defensive battles as 'The Hell of the Somme' again (the 94 German divisions that had fought on the Somme were classed by the British *Official History of the Great War* as being in a 'dire state'). After the war, the German *Official History* acknowledged the losses of killed and wounded during 1916 as 1,400,000; 800,000 of these were accounted for between July and October.

January on the Somme was relatively quiet but losses to minor British operations deprived the army of some useful observation points from which to observe future

For Home Front consumption: a daring patrol near Arras.

Mobile anti-aircraft guns mounted on a lorry.

British assault preparations and, with the certainty of further British attacks, the army was to be ordered back to the Siegfried Stellung. Ludendorff later wrote that 'the decision to retreat was not reached without a painful struggle. It implied a confession of weakness bound to raise the morale of the enemy and lower our own. But it was necessary for military reasons – we had no choice'.

This defensive line, with a depth of between six and eight thousand yards, ran east from Laffaux to Cerny-en-Laonnais on the Chemin des Dames ridge where it joined the front-line defences. Considerable effort had been put into these fortifications, using mass production techniques, which turned out identical components by the thousand. Three belts of barbed wire protected the trenches, each being ten to fifteen yards deep, separated by a five-yard gap from the next. Initial construction was by Russian POWs and later by Belgian civilian conscripts, skilled German craftsmen and troops. Eventually around 65,000 men were employed on this task on a daily basis.

'The retirement to the new positions was code-named Alberich (a malicious dwarf from the Niebelung Saga) and the Army Group was directed to draw up detailed plans for its execution.' Further plans were made to turn the evacuated zone into a desert. 'Not only were all military buildings to be dismantled, depots to be withdrawn, railways to be torn up, craters to be blown in the roads; but so as far as possible, every town and village, every building in them, was to be destroyed by fire or explosive; every tree, even fruit trees, was to be cut down, or "ringed" to ensure that it died; civilians were to be removed; and wells filled up or polluted, though not poisoned.' Leutnant Junger after the war described what had happened: 'every village up to the Siegfried Line was a rubbish heap. Every tree felled, every road mined, every well fouled, every watercourse damned, every cellar blown up or made into a death trap with concealed bombs, all supplies of metal sent back, all rails ripped up, all telephone wires rolled up, everything burnable burned.'

As a hindrance to any advancing troops, and also to economise on food supplies, it was decided to leave between ten and fifteen thousand civilians – almost all were children, their mothers, and the aged. They were to be 'left in Nesle, Ham, Noyon (in the French zone of operations) and a few smaller places in the intact houses for the advancing troops to look after; the remainder were taken away to work in the fields and factories.' The pre-withdrawal programme was scheduled to start on 9 February and end on 15 March, giving the troops five days in which to retire; by 20 March all troops should be in their new positions. Although it was supposed to be a secret withdrawal, prisoners captured by the British indicated that there would be a withdrawal at some point.

The first withdrawal commenced on 14 March and 'over the next two days, the troops withdrew from trench to trench, using sniper fire and machine guns to halt

A false gun position to trick aerial reconnaissance experts into firing onto useless targets.

any pursuit. However, by 16 March, the first full marching day, the main body of the troops were retiring to the Siegfried Stellung and by 18 March four armies were withdrawing on a front of 110 miles followed by six enemy armies. By the end of March, the complete Alberich timetable was in British hands and they were now aware that the original withdrawals were not part of the plan. The whole defence line was not complete; indeed, this was the reason for the need to hold on to certain outpost villages.' By 5 April, the retirement was complete, reducing the amount of line to be defended and increasing the number of men available to counter any future enemy attacks; supply was also easier. However, it was a purely defensive move.

In March, the population of the villages facing the French positions around Arras was moved out and sent, via Switzerland, to French controlled areas as the whole area was a potential battle zone; this action saved the lives of many civilians.

The withdrawal scarcely affected the troops on the Arras Front, except in the very south where troops pulled back towards Neuville Vitasse and Bullecourt. Although 6 Army was remaining on the defensive it was decided to strengthen the positions around Arras to prevent any potential British breakthrough. This entailed new lines of 'deeply echeloned defences, protected with wire entanglements and blockhouses in reinforced concrete.' Between Arras and Douai, besides the old defensive lines of 1914 and 1915, there were three new positions collectively forming the Siegfried Stellung. Coupled with new defensive positions there were also changes to defensive tactics, which provided for immediate counter-attacks using reserves organised at specific points; points at which it was expected that the attacking troops would lose their cohesion after they had taken their initial positions.

Future defence was to be in depth but at the same time elastic. 'Out went deep dugouts and continuous trench lines, to be replaced by concrete bunkers, surrounded by obstacle belts and sited for mutual support. Gone was the rigid holding of the forward trenches packed with infantrymen. In came flexibility, defence in depth, a huge increase in infantry fire power, streamlined command and control and numerous tactical innovations.'

'While the High Command advocated defence, the Entente was gearing up for the offence. Both sides were developing tactics designed to make each other's lives more unpleasant. Fluid defence in depth, rapid deployment of local reserves and not every attack being countered, was countered by the British with the 'box' and 'creeping' barrage with little or no preparation and the night assault. The next battles were to be against the British at Arras and the French on the Chemin des Dames.'

Early in the year 'G.H.Q. began to reckon on the great Entente offensive in France, Macedonia and on the Isonzo for the middle of April.' As a result 'the Army groups of the Crown Prince Rupprecht and the German Crown Prince were strengthened with divisions, artillery and ammunition, and were provided with everything necessary for successful defence.'

Der zweite Feind im Schützengraben.

The second enemy in the trenches - lice.

Gas was an ever present danger in the trenches – troops pose for the family back home with a gas mask ready, just in case.

'During February, identifications from raids had shown that the Canadian Corps was closing in and concentrating on the Vimy plateau, and the increased activity in the British positions was noted, particularly the work carried out on railways and roads, the increase in transport and the arrival of artillery units.' A soldier from the same Bavarian division that had asked the Canadians to not use their artillery as much wrote home in February: 'My dug-out is four metres under the ground, but yet is not quite safe from the British who bombard us like the very devil. Men are constantly being killed or wounded.'

From 19 March, counter-measures were undertaken: reinforcements were brought up in the form of fresh divisions, more heavy artillery, aircraft and machine gun units with six divisions going to *Sixth Army* as a mobile reserve. Behind the lines at Douai 'mountains of shells' were stored and further work was carried out on the defences. However, much of the work was nullified by increase in enemy artillery fire and, even though the enemy artillery barrage had not properly started, many of the new and existing batteries were put out of action; the effects of this counter-battery fire were serious. By 6 April *11 Division* did not possess a single battery able to develop its full fire-power. The harassing fire stopped movement behind the front, leaving the ammunition for the field guns and heavy artillery in Doaui. There was a severe shortage of shells which was particularly disastrous when the British assault took place.

During a trench raid on the morning of 28 March, a soldier from Princess Patricia's Canadian Light Infantry was captured on the ridge. The information he provided under interrogation confirmed an impending attack: 'Behind the entire British lines, from Souchez to Roclincourt, new batteries of field artillery were moving in. More disturbing, infantry companies were being brought up to full strength, a sure sign of impending attack, and each company had been issued with two Vickers machine-guns in addition to their Lewis guns.' An attack was coming but exactly where and when were the unknowns. It would fail of course, as had all the previous attempts, but not without considerable suffering.

There were problems with the existing defences from a defender's point of view. 'The new divisions which were put into the line complained that their predecessors had neglected the trenches and wire; now the bombardment, combined with the bad weather, made adequate repair almost impossible. The strain upon the troops was severe in the extreme' and, even though the enemy artillery barrage had not properly started, many of the new and existing batteries were put out of action.

On the morning of 4 April, the British gas barrage temporarily silenced the greater portion of the artillery. The artillery barrage started just as the gunners of *405 Field Artillery Battalion* were having breakfast of coffee, bread and sausage in their underground shelter. A shell landed directly above them causing the shelter to collapse, burying Kanonier Godry who, upon regaining his senses, scrambled out of the hole left by the shell in the roof. Their position was too dangerous to stay in as the British artillery had zeroed in on their battery with incredible accuracy. He recalled 'although two of our guns had been destroyed and several of our men killed, we were ordered to immediately move the guns to a safer place. This had to be done in a hurry'. They limbered up their gun and moved to the main position on the reverse slope of a hill. Kanonier Godry was the last to leave and decided to use a shortcut to catch them up. This decision meant that he would soon become a victim of the British gas barrage – and, to his friends, a source of amusement. 'Halfway across, a gas shell exploded with a 'pop' about three metres away and I clearly saw the shell break up into a few large fragments from which a large blue foggy cloud emitted and engulfed me. Although I held my breath and carried on running, some of the gas got down me. When I reached the new position I laid my head on the bridge of the gun, feeling awful. Then came the reaction. From out of my eyes, nose and mouth, water was discharging, as if my whole body was trying to get rid of all its liquid matter. But my comrades thought it funny and were rolling about laughing.'

Two of the defending divisions were the chief recipients of the gas: while *11 Division* suffered few casualties, the casualty rate in *14 Bavarian Division* was much greater. This had a demoralising effect on their future combat performance, so much so that they surrendered more readily when the enemy attacked on 9 April.

But it was not only the British who were attacking: the whole purpose of the British attacks had been to take the focus to the Arras front so that the main attack could occur on the Chemin des Dames. However, the start of both offensives was pre-empted by an assault on French positions. After a violent artillery bombardment on 4 April, an attack was launched on a front of three and a half miles, with the right flank on Sapigneul, just south of the Aisne. It was initially successful, attaining the Aisne–Marne Canal, 700 yards behind the French line, in the centre of the attack zone. French counterattacks gradually recovered the lost ground; by 12 April almost the whole of it was again in French hands. However, while no territory was gained, the attack plans for the French offensive were captured. Although General Nivelle knew about the loss by 7 April, two days before the launch of the British offensive, he decided that the operations already scheduled would continue.

In order to improve their defensive positions around Arras, *6 Army* 'wanted to make a rectification of its line by means of a local advance at Souchez…at the beginning of April.' On 6 April Ludendorff came to the conclusion that a great British offensive was imminent at Arras. Now OHL knew that they faced a threat on two fronts. As a result the operation at Souchez was abandoned and Ludendorff requested Group Headquarters to bring up their reserves in anticipation of an attack – which materialised on 9 April. The divisions that constituted the second and third waves were moved up by *6 Army* but by the start of the attack were not close enough to the front to be effective.

The enemy bombardment caused severe damage, reducing the forward trenches to lines of shell-holes, while 'those in the rear suffered only a little less seriously…the wire, bad to begin with, disappeared altogether in many places, and fresh stocks to repair it could not be brought forward…section by section, the defences were systematically reduced'. However, other necessities besides wire could also not be brought up: 'it took six hours to bring up rations from the regimental headquarters to the front line, a distance of about a mile in most cases, and towards the end of the bombardment none could be moved in certain sections'.

As well as high explosive, thousands of gas shells were fired by the British artillery, affecting their opponents severely. After four days of being shelled by gas, one soldier noted in his diary that one officer had been killed and several were ill because of it:

Feldgottesdienst hinterd.Front b. Arras.

Landsturm Infantry Battalion Limburg at a field service behind the Arras front.

'the sad point is that the English gas is almost odourless and can only be seen by the practised eye on escaping from the shell. The gas steals steadily over the ground in a bluish haze and kills everyone who does not draw his mask over his face as quick as lightning before taking a breath…Our people say that things weren't as bad at Verdun as here.'

With such an intense barrage, whole units disappeared from view and control: 'from the 6th to the 8th (of April) the *51st Regiment* had no news at all from one of its companies in first line (sic). On the latter morning a patrol got through to it, to return with a report that the defences were destroyed, that the men had been without sleep and almost without food since the beginning of the bombardment, and that losses were heavy…the *10th Grenadier Regiment* in the same division…had 181 casualties during the bombardment'. While troops using the deep dugouts were safe from the shellfire, the entrances were not and many were blown in.

'Enemy counter battery fire was so effective that one division reported that it did not have a single battery able to perform at full capacity. And neither the… "mountains of ammunition" nor the extra heavy artillery arrived at the front, so that when the enemy attacked there was a general shortage of ammunition with which to delay the attacking forces.'

Facing the British were strong defences, especially south of the Neuville St.-Vaast to Bailleul road; after the first system of trenches there were three or four further lines from seventy-five to one hundred and fifty yards apart, linked by communication trenches at least every hundred yards; behind that was a support line and the formidable Siegfried Stellung. South of the River Scarpe there was a very strong, heavily wired reserve line, about three miles from the front, the Wancourt-Feuchy line, while on the northern side it curved back up to five miles. From the river at Athies to Farbus ran the intermediate Point du Jour line along the steep eastern slope of Vimy Ridge; behind that was a newly constructed reserve line, the Drocourt-Quéant switch. Holding these positions were troops of above average quality: *11, 17, 18, 23, 24, 79 Divisions* and *220 Reserve Division* together with *14 Bavarian* and *1 Bavarian Reserve Divisions*.

Ludendorff recorded his impression of the British attack in his memoirs: 'on the 9th, after a short but extraordinarily intense artillery preparation, our army encountered a powerful attack, led by tanks, on both sides of the Scarpe. Some of our advanced divisions gave way. The neighbouring divisions which stood firm suffered heavy losses. The enemy succeeded before noon in reaching our battery positions and seizing heights which dominated the country far to the east. The counter-attacking divisions were not there to throw the enemy back, only portions of the troops could be brought up by motor transport. The situation was extremely critical, and might have had far-reaching and serious consequences if the enemy had pushed further forward. But the British contented themselves with their great success and did not continue the attack, at least not on April 9th.'

The British attack ruined Ludendorff's birthday and left him feeling deeply depressed, but, after talking to officers who had taken part in the fighting, he found that the new defensive ideas and principles were sound. However, he recorded that 'the battle of Arras on April 9th was a bad beginning for the decisive struggle' of the year, and that it threw all calculations to the wind.

The Battles of Arras 1917 are best known by the loss of Vimy Ridge, which happened in the first phase. There were several distinct phases: 9 to 14 April, the First Battle of the Scarpe and the Battle of Vimy Ridge; 23 and 24 April, the Second Battle of the Scarpe; 28 and 29 April, the Battle of Arleux; 3 and 4 May, the Third Battle of the Scarpe, with the loss of Fresnoy; 3 to 17 May, the very desperate Battle of Bullecourt, fought after a first unsuccessful (British) attack on 11 April, with the fighting lasting until after the end of May.

After the war, Ludendorff summarised the battle for Arras. The battle continued with the British attacking 'again at the same spot from the 10th onwards in great strength, but not really on a grand scale. They extended their offensive on both sides, especially to the south, as far as Bullecourt. On the 11th they took Monchy, and during the following night we evacuated Vimy ridge. April 23rd and 28th and May 3rd were again days of severe fighting, and in the intervals sharp local engagements took place. The battles continued; we launched minor counter-attacks, which were successful, but also suffered slight losses of ground here and there.' Then the French opened their offensives in Champagne and on the Aisne. Many years after the war when Ludendorff wrote his memoirs he could see little if any strategic point to the battle for Arras – a battle with a higher casualty rate than the Somme

In his autobiography, 'Out of My Life', Marshall Von Hindenburg, Ludendorff's commanding officer, described the British attack as being more serious. 'On April 9th the English attack at Arras gave the signal for the enemy's great spring offensive. The attack was prepared for days with the fury of masses of enemy artillery and trench mortars. There was nothing of the surprise tactics that Nivelle had used in the October of the previous year. ... The English swept over our first, second and third lines. Groups of strongpoints were overwhelmed or silenced after heroic resistance. Masses of artillery were lost. Our defensive system had apparently failed ! ... The evening report of the 9th April revealed a rather dark picture ... many shadows - little light. In such cases more light must be sought. A ray appeared, a tiny flickering ray. The English did not seem to have known how to exploit the success they had gained to the full. This was a piece of luck for us, as so often before! ... I knew that our reinforcements were hastening to the battlefield and that trains were hastening that way.'

9 April, when the British and Canadian forces attacked, was punctuated by squalls of rain, sleet and snow with a long and heavy snow-shower at night. At times the westerly wind blew the snow into the defenders' eyes, making it difficult to see, but between the showers the weather was bright and clear. Although the bombardment had battered the trenches almost beyond recognition and cut the wire to shreds, the deep dugouts were full of men. The defence can be divided into two distinct types: troops who fought according to the new defence scheme and those who fought using the traditional methods of defence. The new defence rested on island positions which generally quickly surrendered or were abandoned while the traditional commanders 'caught up the retiring troops and gave them a rallying position, which was reinforced by any available garrisons of strong points in rear', often successfully delaying the attacking force. This new style of defence relied upon the swift arrival of reserves or the specialised counter-attack divisions, but, as these were too far away, the defence collapsed.

Within the defences of Vimy Ridge were numerous caves, connected by tunnels, some of them believed to have been used in the Wars of Religion during the 16th Century. From these caves, exits had been cut into the front-line trenches so their garrisons, sheltered up to fifty feet below the surface, could emerge fresh to meet

The result of an Allied artillery barrage.

the assault when the bombardment stopped or lifted. The defences were shallow by comparison to positions further south, but were still strong, being protected by deep belts of wire, and further back the plateau 'was chequered with elaborate redoubts and concrete machine-gun emplacements and along the upper edge of the woods on the eastern face of the ridge' were a number of batteries in concrete casemates.

From observation posts on the dominating Hill 135 and Hill 145, fresh evidence of the British preparations could be seen every morning, but little effort was made to disrupt the build-up. This lack of activity led the British into thinking that the ridge was about to be evacuated. However, the opposite was true; 16 Bavarian Division was scheduled to attack the British at the northern end of the ridge and take their positions but, as the wind was unfavourable for the use of gas shells, on which the attack was based, it was cancelled.

Both the shelling and the weather impacted on conditions on the ridge. The ridge is chalk, but is covered in a layer of clay and decomposed chalk mixed with fine sand. After being pounded by nearly a million shells, the surface was 'a wilderness of clammy mud. The sides of trenches collapsed on the burst of a shell, and as the water could not drain quickly, they became quagmires of slime, in places knee-deep.' As a result 'the forward defence system lost all continuity, and in places its trenches could no longer be distinguished. The garrisons of the deep dug-outs, situated about 120 yards apart in the first and second trenches, were isolated during daylight.' Positions further back fared little better.

This isolation made the supply of food to the front-line garrisons extremely difficult. 'Ration parties often took six hours to make a journey which had formerly taken a quarter of an hour, and the food on arrival was cold and filthy.' Movement was so difficult at times that many front line 'companies went without fresh food for two or three days at a time.'

There were only five regiments (equivalent to one and a half divisions) facing four full strength Canadian divisions, and, while the Canadian units were generally well rested and up to full strength, the opposite was true on the ridge. Four of the regiments had been in the line for at least five weeks and many of their companies were down to a rifle strength of between 70 and 80 men, which meant that the 15,000 men of the Canadian Corps faced only 5,000 defenders; in reserve, up to six miles in the rear, were a further 3,000 men against 12,000 Entente rifles. At Doaui, between twelve and fifteen miles away, were two divisions in 6 Army reserve. Getting any reserves to the front would take between two and four hours. If the Entente could keep the time and day of the attack secret, there would not be time to halt the initial rush of the attack.

During the night of 8/9 April there was little to alarm the sentries even though 30,000 men of the Canadian Corps had assembled on a front of nearly four miles, many within a hundred yards of the remains of the wire their artillery had carefully destroyed. Many men were waiting in tunnels that opened out into the front lines. At 0530 hours, the British artillery opened fire and two mines were exploded under the front-line. After three minutes' rapid fire on the first trenches, the fire moved on 100 yards every three minutes. Simultaneously all battery positions and ammunition dumps were bombarded with gas shells and high explosives. Because of the gas, the horses could not move the guns or bring up ammunition; the batteries quickly ran out of shells. This, coupled with the damaged telephone cables and the destruction of most of the observation posts meant that the response to the rocket signals from the beleaguered front line positions was very feeble.

In some places, the advance was so rapid that garrisons could not leave their deep dugouts, although in others machine gunners did their jobs successfully before being over-run. The further the British advanced, the stiffer the resistance they faced, with increasing losses among the attackers. However, in some cases, although the machine gunners fought with courage, many of the troops were dazed by the barrage and attack and appeared happy to be taken prisoner. Two independent counter-attacks were launched without any success.

In most cases, the artillery preparation had been sufficient to allow the Canadian troops to leave their tunnels and successfully advance. One exception occurred at Tottenham Tunnel, in range of a strongpoint that had been rebuilt after having been destroyed earlier. At 400 yards the machine guns fired directly into the advancing Canadians accounting for around half of them, and attempts to rush the position were halted by the undamaged wire. Close by, persistent sniping and a counter-attack drove back the most advanced troops with heavy loss.

However, by around 0700 hours, from the Labyrinth salient to Gunner crater, except for a short strip on Hill 145, the entire front defence system had been lost to the Canadians. The garrison on Hill 145 was able to hold out because the wire had not been destroyed, allowing the sheltered troops time to occupy their positions; the garrison would hold out for a further day and a half.

Much of the ground had been previously fought over and revealed macabre sights to the advancing troops. Uncovered by shell-fire were the remains of dead French soldiers from 1915, complete with their rifles and bayonets.

As the first wave of Canadian troops consolidated their positions, the support troops moved forward through spasmodic artillery shelling that caused a number of casualties. By 0830 hours the shelling of the advancing troops had ceased completely because no infantry remained to send up rockets for assistance; the artillery could get no news because 'all telephone cables leading forward, including one buried 6 ft. deep, had been broken, and patrols sent forward could bring no enlightenment.'

After the war the Reichsarchiv volume on the battle described the strength of the artillery barrage on *261 Reserve Regiment*. Those who survived the initial barrage watched the positions they had just vacated 'disappear in a veil of smoke and fumes, while the fiery flashes of grenades and mines illuminated the battlefield with blood-red streaks of fire.' However, unlike their compatriots on other parts of the front *261 Reserve Regiment* incredulously watched the British troops advance, as they had at the Somme, 'attempting laboriously and step by step to traverse the slimy waste between their own positions and the German line of craters.' They were also able to send up flares for artillery support and use the surviving machine guns on their attackers: 'crackling into life…they found their targets. Forward of *5 Company* the British corpses accumulate and form small hills of khaki.'

To their left, the British preparatory artillery had been effective in destroying the defenders' machine guns, allowing the attacking troops to move forward against the two defending companies. The words of the Reichsarchiv historian report on the fate of the companies: 'Defending themselves against attack from all sides and no longer hoping for help from outside, *9* and *11 Companies*' bled to death. Only five men managed to make their way back to the rear of the ridge.'

Von der englischen Front im Westen.
Canadische Truppen erhalten die letzten Instruktionen zu ihrem bevor-
stehenden Sturmangriff.

Canadian troops undergoing instruction about their targets during the coming offensive.

262 Reserve Regiment on the left flank of *261 Reserve Regiment* suffered the same treatment; the British attack was both furious and fast. Fusilier Schroeder described what happened to him, and probably many of his countryman, during the attack. 'In the morning, tired and back from night duty, we lay down with the words : "Now let us put the blankets over our heads and sleep." Suddenly there was heavy drumfire. The day sentries shouted, "Outside, the British are coming!"

We jumped up, all tiredness gone, for our country and our lives were at stake. While I was handing out hand-grenades, the shooting had already started. The English – they are Canadian troops – had broken through on our left and were already rolling up our own position. My corporal told me to go down into the dug-out and fetch the box with the egg-shaped hand-grenades but on the way back, when I had gone up half of the thirty-two rungs, the corporal suddenly shouted: "Come up on the left, the British have already passed the trench!" So I dropped the egg-grenades and went up. I noticed I was alone, only a dead comrade was lying on the edge of the trench in a grotesque way. Then I ventured beyond the edge of the trench, and everywhere, left and right and forward, I saw only Britishers.'

Fusilier Schroeder now had to make a choice; fight, surrender, try and get back to his own lines or stay put. The area was swarming with enemy troops and, realising the danger of his position, he chose to stay put. With discretion being the better part of valour he 'lay down beside his dead comrade and played dead too, while more assault waves came pouring over him'. Everything was fine until a soldier decided to investigate the two dead soldiers. When Schroeder saw his comrade being prodded with a bayonet he decided to move, at which point the Canadian told him to come on and he climbed out. Fortunately the soldier only asked if he was wounded. When he pretended that he did not understand English, the man ran off to join his unit, leaving him alone.

Once again Fusilier Schroeder had a decision to make; this time he decided to run for his own lines. 'I ran in the direction of the Pimple, towards the positions of the *261st Regiment*. But an Englishman jumped up and fired at me. I was hit in the right forearm. After that, while I was wandering around in a wounded state, my pal Cordes jumped out from some cover where he had managed to remain unhurt. We took each other by the hand and ran planlessly among the dead'. Schroeder's luck continued to hold when they found a Canadian-occupied dugout where they found six soldiers playing cards, who paid no attention to them whatever. When the game was over, however, a medical orderly came over to them. '"Hullo, Fritz," he said. "Are you wounded?" I nodded, and he examined me and said, "Not good." Then he bandaged me and gave me something to eat and drink.' Schroeder and his friend were not the only survivors of their company. While he waited to be taken to a rear area, gradually more and more of his regiment showed up. After a rest, the medic decided it was time for him to move on. 'After I had regained some strength, the Englishman took me by the hand and took me to the main dressing station, where I was examined by a doctor'. He was then released and sent on his way to a big camp behind the front, where he found several comrades. Fusilier Schroeder was now a prisoner of war, like many thousands of his countrymen.

Such was the speed of the advance that many units were surrounded, leaving the officers with a difficult decision to make – surrender or try and fight their way back. Leutnant Schlensog of *51 Prussian Infantry Regiment* had to make this decision. Surrounded, out of ammunition and realising that a breakout using bayonets would only result in the deaths of the remainder of his men, he opted for surrender. He recounted that: 'As soon as we stopped firing we were overrun by the enemy who were not interested in us as individuals, but for what possessions we had. Watches, rings, iron crosses and whatever else was worth taking they took from us as if it was their God-given right. As if robbery was their major line of work.'

'Group Vimy was now a shattered force. It had all happened so quickly. Questing Canadians, searching the dug-outs…for lurking snipers, found food on the tables, bottles of soda water and wine in the cupboards.' Casualties were heavy: *261 Reserve*

Regiment had lost 900 officers and men killed, wounded and missing, and would not be fit for further action for many months. *3 Battalion* of *263 Reserve Regiment*, which had arrived in the line just before the attack to relieve *2 Battalion*, was lost entirely except for a handful of men and one officer. The situation was dangerous for the stability of the front, as Crown Prince Rupprecht wrote in his diary: 'I doubt that we can recapture the Vimy Ridge…This leads to the question: is there any sense in continuing the war?'

The story was similar along the whole front. If they had had time, and a clear view through the sleet, the defenders in front of Thélus would have seen Canadian troops advancing through fully cut wire, over almost completely destroyed forward trenches, with a barrage moving steadily ahead of them. However, only when the barrage had moved on were they able to emerge from their deep dugouts. But it was too late; the assault waves were already in their rear. 'In the past, they had attacked these unsuspecting forward troops, forcing them to turn back, but this time ineffectual defensive fire, and the presence of the tunnels, permitted the next waves to advance safely and engage the inhabitants of the dug-outs.'

Musketier Kraft, a seventeen-year-old from Kiel, was one of the soldiers trapped in a dugout by the speed of the Canadian advance. His survival depended upon luck and his behaviour, as he found out when he and his comrades surrendered. As they rested on their bunks with the artillery shells pounding their positions, the electricity failed. After lighting candles, the sergeant, who led the way, ordered them up the stairs. Upon reaching the top he yelled 'Tommies' and fell back down the stairs dead. The situation was not good. If they waited, they would die when the Canadians threw grenades down into the dugout. He later recounted: 'We all panicked and ran back into the cave and threw ourselves down with arms over our heads , fearing a bomb at any second. Then one of our "old hands" (he was twenty-two) came down the steps and told us to abandon our weapons and come up the steps one at a time as the position was hopeless, the English were all over us.' Kraft was one of the lucky ones, unlike the defiant corporal who walked up in front of him. As they reached the entrance, the corporal spat on the floor, only to be greeted by a baseball bat on the head. Expecting the same welcome, Kraft covered his head with his hands and closed his eyes but nothing happened; perhaps it was because he looked very young. Opening his eyes, he viewed his captors and realised that they were Canadians: 'Looking at the soldiers, I noticed that they all had their faces blackened. I was prodded in the stomach by one with a bayonet and told to keep my hands on my head. One of the soldiers wore no helmet and had no hair, apart from a small tuft on the top of his head. He also had white and red paint on his face and was very fearsome looking. I then realised that he was a Red Indian, and our captors were Canadians.'

The Kaiser and Hindenburg on the Arras front in 1917.

In the late morning, to the south of the ridge where the attack had not been held up, a sudden change in the weather gave rise to a curious occurrence. After the war, Franz Behrmann recorded what he had seen: 'the cessation of the snowstorm lifted the veil which had till now hidden the landscape, and we saw a remarkable sight. The air was suddenly clean and clear, filled with spring sunshine. The high ground about Thélus was covered with English storm troops standing about in large groups. The officers could easily be distinguished waving their short sticks in the air and hurrying from group to group to give instructions. For a few minutes the artillery fire almost ceased on both sides and complete silence fell upon the battlefield, as if all were lost in wonder. The battle itself seemed to hold its breath.'

As is common in war, uncertainty breeds rumour and exaggeration. The Canadian reconnaissance of Willerval was one such incident; initially successful, the two patrols soon ran into more opposition than they were able to deal with and beat a hasty retreat with some loss. Although the two patrols numbered less than twenty and had been beaten back, this was quickly amplified to 'a strong force of English Cavalry (that) had broken through into Willerval.' So seriously was the threat taken that *I Battalion* of *225 Reserve Regiment*, newly arrived in nearby Arleux, was ordered to recapture the village at once, even though the cavalry had long gone.

In all areas of the attack the British and Canadian troops pushed forward, trying to keep to their allotted timetable. 'On the right of the British attack on the 9th April stood the *18th Reserve Division*. It faced the left brigade of the (British) 21st Division – the only brigade of that division which took part in the original attack – the 30th Division and the right brigade of the 56th Division.' *18th Reserve* 'was the most fortunate of the German divisions. Its main defences were the two trenches of the strong Hindenburg or Siegfried system, though its third trench, the Artillerieschutsistellung, was shallow and without shelters. All three regiments were in line, each having two battalions in the three trenches mentioned, and the third in reserve. On the German left, the *84th Reserve Regiment* lost a portion of the Hindenburg Line on the afternoon of the 9th April, but recovered it by a counter-attack next evening. The *86th Reserve Regiment*, in the centre, repulsed the attack of the 30th Division. It was only the *31st Reserve Regiment*, on the right, which suffered seriously in the attack of the 9th. Its right turned by the fall of Neuville Vitasse, it formed a flank facing north in a communication trench south of and parallel to the Neuville-Wancourt road. On the 10th April it was ordered to withdraw to a new line running about a thousand yards north-west of Wancourt and Guémappe; but the troops in the salient immediately south of Neuville were nearly all mopped up by the bombers of the 56th Division. Early on the 10th, a battalion of the *121st Reserve Regiment* was placed at the disposal of the *38th Reserve Division*.'

'This battalion belonged to the *26th Reserve Division,* which had just been relieved at Bullecourt. All the remainder of the division had gone back to rest areas, but this unit happened to be still on the platform at Cagnicourt awaiting a train, and was marched north into the battle. Later in the day two battalions of the *26th Division*, one of the so-called "counter-attack divisions", were added as a reserve.'

'The *18th Reserve Division* was driven back but never really broken, as were those further north. It was left in action until the 14th April, and its casualties were not very high: according to its own account, 62 officers and 1,702 other ranks.' But not all divisions were as lucky as *18 Reserve Division*. With its left flank resting on the Neuville to Wancourt road, *17 Division* held the line from Neuville Vitasse to Tilloy les Mofflaines, a sector about to be attacked by the British 3, 14 and 56 Divisions. Casualties would be high.

'The *163rd Regiment*, on the left, had three companies annihilated at Neuville Vitasse. On the evening of the 9th April it repulsed the British attack against the Wancourt–Feuchy line, between the Arras–Cambrai and Neuville–Wancourt roads. On the morning of the 10th, however, news came that the *11th Division* had retired from this line further north. The divisional commander, General von Reuter, therefore ordered a withdrawal to the half-prepared Monchy village position.

Screened by a snowstorm, the 350 survivors of the *163rd Regiment* fell back. They joined two companies of the centre regiment, the *162nd,* in the sunken Monchy–Guémappe road, north of the point where it crossed the Cambrai road. The reserve battalion of the *162nd* was placed on the Monchy–Roeux road, facing west and northwest, and commanding the Scarpe valley. It was the remnants of these two regiments that held up the advance of the British (37th Division) on the 10th April.'

Without reinforcements to contain the enemy attack, the situation would inevitably deteriorate, but not until the afternoon did the first arrive, advancing in artillery formation from Boiry Notre Dame, in the shape of a battalion of *3 Bavarian Division* that had been rushed from the Lille district. With divisional artillery having almost ceased to exist, the sight of a new divisional artillery crossing open ground at a gallop and unlimbering behind Monchy le Preux raised the defenders' spirits. As one participant recorded: 'There was a great arc of our batteries on a wide front behind our endangered positions. It was a most memorable and magnificent battle picture, lit by the evening sun.' Its timely arrival would mean a hot reception for the British attack the next day.

Reinforcements were on the way. Behind the lines, near Doaui, Leutnant Junger, who had arrived back from leave on 9 April to find out about the losses, and his men prepared to join the battle the next day. Their job was to set up an observation post in Fresnoy. After the war he wrote about what happened: 'I took a few men and explored the western outskirts of the village and found a cottage, in whose roof I had a look-out post made that commanded the front. We took the cellar as our dwelling-place, and in the course of making room there we came upon a sack of potatoes, a very welcome addition to our scanty provisions.' His friend who was holding Willerval with just one platoon sent him some wine from supplies found in the village. Not wanting to miss an opportunity, Junger 'equipped an expedition furnished with perambulators and similar means of transport to secure this treasure.' But their luck was out – the British had got there first. The presence of the wine had caused some problems, as his friend later told him: 'after the discovery of a large cellar of red wine a drinking bout had started, which, in spite of the attack then being made on the village, it had been extremely difficult to bring to a close.'

Casualties had been heavy after lengthy actions such as the defence of Tilloy and the holding of 3 (British) Division at the Wancourt–Feuchy line, so heavy that, although units were pulled back to hold other parts of the line, it was necessary for them to be relieved by fresher units such as *1 Battalion* of *17 Bavarian Regiment* from *3 Bavarian Division*. The casualties of one division, *17 Reserve Division*, stand as an example of the level of loss experienced: 79 officers and 2,700 other ranks between 9 and 11 April.

Further proof of the intensity of the fighting is given by *11 Division:* on 9 April, it was attacked by 12 and 15 (British) Divisions and the right wing of 9 (British) Division. Fighting was severe and two battalions of *38 Regiment* were destroyed.

In the centre, the front line trenches of *51 Regiment* were overrun, and the Wancourt–Feuchy line was evacuated on the morning of 10 April on the order of a staff officer, given without the approval of the divisional commander. It fell back to the new Monchy–Roeux line, and was relieved in front of Pelves by *3Bn. 125 Regiment* of *26 Division*. On the right were *10 Grenadier Regiment*, that, contrary to the general practice, had two battalions in line. 'The support companies of these battalions made a prolonged and gallant defence of the railway embankment on the 10th, but had very few survivors'. The reserve battalion, with that of *38 Regiment*, held the front from Roeux station to the Scarpe, and repulsed 4 (British) Division's attempted advance from Fampoux. Losses for *11 Division* were 105 officers and 3,154 other ranks in the two days' fighting and, of this total, British Intelligence estimates suggest 2,200 were captured.

The casualties were heavy, but the divisions had done their best – except one that had met the attack of 9 and 34 (British) Divisions, and later of 4 (British) Division; Ludendorff suggested that *14 Bavarian Division* had failed. This is a harsh judgment – as even the British Official History implies: 'It should in fairness be said that it had received the worst of the gas bombardment, which seems to have affected its morale, in addition to the actual casualties caused. Its losses are not given, but it is known that the British took 2,800 prisoners from it. If, therefore, its ratio of prisoners to total casualties was similar to that of its neighbour, the 11th, its losses in two days would be over 4,000.' In the same period *1 Bavarian Reserve Division* reported a loss of 112 officers and 3,021 other ranks. *2nd Bavarian Reserve Regiment*, part of this latter division, held up the advance of 51 British Division on the Point du Jour line before being pushed back to the outskirts of Bailleul the next morning. Another unit of the division, *1 Bavarian Reserve Regiment*, suffered very heavily, being reduced to 150 of all ranks.

The conditions made it difficult to form and man a new front. Reinforcements were a varied group – some from resting, some from distant places like Lille, and some from the general reserve; they were 'flung hurriedly into the battle-line, to be attached to divisions holding the front when the latter were still in a state to continue the struggle, and to relieve them as quickly as possible when they were not. The least mauled troops of the original front-line division were left in for a longer period than those which had suffered severely and fought on, intermingled with the fresh troops. It was fortunate …that the attack became almost as disorganized as the defence', giving the defending battle-line 'time to steady itself, to consolidate new or half-prepared positions, and to put its system of ammunition supply into order.'

Continuing British pressure caused further problems. The bridgehead over the Cojeul river was held by *84 and 86 Reserve Regiments* of *18 Reserve Division*; these regiments were in danger of being cut off and the decision was made, in the evening of 11 April, by *Gruppe Arras,* to evacuate them. They withdrew in the early hours of 12 April, but the British advance guard managed to get in among them and make their withdrawal to the Guémappe-Riegel line more difficult. This new line had been hastily dug; it ran across the commanding Wancourt ridge.

The fighting for Monchy was also hard. 'The *23rd Bavarian Regiment,* in the centre, was broken by a "mass of British troops" from Monchy (i.e. the leading waves of two battalions). The extreme left of the *18th Bavarian Regiment* swung back and took the advance in enfilade. Thereupon it came to a halt, but supports "pouring out of Monchy" (which could only be the rear waves of the same two battalions) carried it forward to some 500 yards behind the original Bavarian line. The *23rd Bavarian Regiment,* however, claims to have given way "elastically", so that the I/R. Newfoundland and 1/Essex were caught in a trap.'

Unteroffizier Bernardini of *23 Bavarian Regiment,* a twenty-one year old veteran who held the Iron Cross, first and second class, was holding out in a house on the main street with a few of his men. Arriving in Monchy during the night to find the village very badly damaged, they were ordered to occupy the western part and immediately set about fortifying the houses before the British arrived. He described what happened: 'Early in the morning we came under heavy artillery fire and the English attacked the village. As dawn broke a tank came rattling across the cobbles of the main street, closely followed by the English infantry who obviously felt quite safe. Hidden in this house, I ordered my men to hold their fire until I gave the word. I waited until the tank had got past and then we opened up with everything we had. The English were totally caught by surprise and many were shot down by our hail of fire. The rest scattered. Then we found out that the English had broken through at both ends of the village. Afraid that we would be cut off, we fought our way back to the east side and made good our escape.'

'The reserve battalion of the *23rd Bavarian Regiment* pushed straight forward from the rear position on which it was working. The left of the *18th,* assisted by survivors of the right battalion of the *23rd,* formed a barrier between Monchy and the unfortunate British troops east of it. A battalion of the *17th Bavarian Regiment* from Boiry moved up on the British right and joined hands with further surviving companies of the "elastic" 23rd. Counter-attacked from three sides, 150 British surrendered, but the majority tried to get back to Monchy.' This was not possible and the retreating British were shot down at leisure.

Many troops were facing tanks for the first time that day. Musketier Keyser noted how effective they were because of their firepower: 'when it was directly opposite

Zum frommen Andenken im Gebete
an den Ehrwürdigen Herrn

Josef Mayr

**Kandidat der Theologie u. Akolyth
im Erzb. Klerikalseminar Freising
Oekonomssohn v. Happing Pf. Pang**

Unteroffizier und Offiziersaspirant b.
2. Bayr. Res.-Jnfantr.-Reg. 2. Komp.

Jnhaber des Eisernen Kreuzes

der am 9. April (Ostermontag) 1917, nach
26monatlicher treuer und gewissenhafter
Pflichterfüllung infolge schwerer Verwun-
dung durch eine Granate im Alter von 27
Jahren 5 Monaten den Heldentod für sein
Vaterland gestorben ist.

R. I. P.

Was weint Jhr, Eltern, Geschwister meine
    Lieben ?
Weil ich nicht länger bin bei Euch geblieben?
Es ist nicht weit, blickt auf zum Stern,
Dort oben wohn' ich gar nicht fern !
Weil ich früh geschieden, vor des Altares
    Stufen ?
Auch Euch wird einst der Vater rufen;
Wie bald, wie schnell verrinnt die Zeit:
Jhr seid bei mir, ich bin bei Euch — dort
    in der Ewigkeit

Buchdruckerei „Wendelstein" Rosenheim.

Unteroffizier and Offizieraspirant Josef Mayr, a theological student from Happing, winner of the Iron Cross 2nd class, died from severe wounds received during the shelling of his positions on 9 April 1917 while serving with *2 Bavarian Reserve Infantry Regiment.*

our trench the thing (a tank) started shooting at us with eight machine guns. Our rifle fire was useless against it and we had to withdraw.' Not only its firepower, but also its cross country abilities impressed Feldwebel Speck. His regiment had been ordered to fill the gap left by the retreating *17 Bavarian Regiment* and finding good cover behind the hedges on the main road, watched the British advance over half a kilometre away; a tank then appeared. Everyone was affected – as he noted: 'We stared aghast as slowly a tank crept towards us. At fifty metres we opened fire with rifles and machine guns but, as it got within thirty metres of us, it suddenly turned off to the right towards the Bavarians. We clapped and cheered! And standing up we shot from the hip at the tank.' It was then that they were given a demonstration of its capabilities – the tank turned back towards them and advanced. They hoped that the large ditch would provide them with safety, but they were dismayed to see it tip into the ditch, then straighten itself out, and head towards them. The tank got within five metres and then stopped without firing.

Seeing their chance, some men left their positions and attacked the tank with grenades, while those who held their position joined in firing at the tank. Then the tank returned to life: 'the tank tracks began to move and the tank crew opened up with murderous machine-gun fire which was slowly directed along *1st Company* trench. Those that were not killed instantly, screamed as they lay there wounded.' When the tank fired upon another trench, panic set in: 'everyone from *1st* and *3rd Companies* jumped out of the trench and ran the fastest race of his life, pursued by the merciless tank machine-gun fire which cut down many men as if it were a rabbit-shoot'. Such was the effect on experienced soldiers.

General von Wenninger, the divisional commander, decided to attack Monchy that afternoon. The bad news arrived about 3pm when the infantry was moving up. The artillery commander reported 'that the ammunition railhead at Vitry was under heavy fire, that the destination of the trains had been altered to Corbehem, that the ammunition available was sufficient only to hold off one more big British attack, and that owing to the state of the roads the supplies could not be replenished during the night if they were expended now.' The history of *18 Bavarian Regiment* admits that the British placed an impenetrable barrage east of Monchy so no attack could get through. Close by, *26 Division* continued to hold its narrow front astride the Scarpe and *18 Division* its wider one between Roeux Station and the railway north of Gavrelle.

Not all counter-attacks were unsuccessful. A company of Seaforth Highlanders had successfully pushed back the untried youngsters of *11 Company, 31 Regiment*, opposite Hyberdad Redoubt, when the Battalion Commander formed the survivors for a counter-attack. At 3pm a bugle sounded and the men advanced into a hail of fire but no artillery. The enemy fell back towards Fampoux which further galvanized the counter-attack troops. Quickly they reached their previous positions and then had to decide whether to continue or dig-in. But some British troops were not prepared to pull back. Otto Noack, on reaching the front line, turned round to see his friends trying to draw his attention to the right. 'I turned round and found myself staring with fascination straight down the barrel of a revolver which was emitting small puffs of smoke. There were at least two puffs before I reacted to the danger and dodged out of the way. It dawned on me that the man behind the revolver was wearing an English helmet and there were two others with him.' They were only a few metres away. One of his comrades landed at his feet and they both threw grenades in the direction of their enemy. As the smoke cleared, he jumped into their position to find them dead. The counter-attack had been successful and the position was held throughout the day and night.

Crown Prince Rupprecht, aware that there could be further attacks, ordered a further withdrawal that was to be completed by dawn on 13 April. During the night of 11/12 April 'the remaining civilians in the villages near the third line were hurried away from their homes, and every available vehicle was used to carry back stores. The artillery withdrew, leaving only a small proportion in position. After dusk on the 12th the front-line battalions and the last guns in action slipped away, leaving only patrols to offer a semblance of opposition to the pursuit'. As the troops were leaving, the counter-attack troops were arriving with their own field artillery and the missing heavy artillery. On 18 April, these troops were to face the British 1 Corps and Canadian Corps when they attacked from the Vimy and Lorette Ridges.

As well as underground tunnels, mining operations and infantry attacks the battle was also fought above the trenches. The air over the battlefield was patrolled by Baron von Richthofen and his 'flying circus', who were responsible for shooting down seventy-five British aircraft between 4 and 8 April, including twenty-eight on the first day of the battle. To the British air force this period was known as 'Bloody April'. However, sometimes the British fliers got the upper hand. One serious loss was Leutnant W Frankl, credited with nineteen victories and awarded the *Pour le Merite* and Iron Cross 1st and 2nd Class, who was killed on 8 April. His loss was watched by Musketier Keyser while he was enjoying a walk with a comrade: 'The weather was clear and soon there were planes about. We saw the usual dog-fight which regularly happened in the afternoon and saw an English plane fall out of the sky, and then another one which somersaulted over and over before hitting the ground…Unfortunately it was one of ours…Leutnant Frankl…lying still in front of us. Solemnly we went back to the village.'

Further south, the British Fifth Army was tasked with providing assistance to the Arras attacks; the area chosen was Bullecourt. Although Fifth Army had been successful in its attacks against villages from Croiselles to Doignies on 2 April, the time left before the start of the offensive gave insufficient time to cut the wire and, when inspected, no gaps could be found, the troops reporting that the wire was thirty yards deep to the east of Bullecourt; as a result the attack was postponed; similarly the attack on the next day. Finally, in the early hours of 11 April, Australian troops again took up position in the snow to wait for the attack. They waited for the tanks that, due to mechanical problems or machine gun and shell fire, were able to offer little assistance, although the garrisons of both Riencourt and Hendecourt fell back under the attack of two tanks and the following infantry.

The advancing Australian infantry suffered heavy casualties, from troops who stood their ground and fought grimly, but did make progress, even when the wire was not cut. However, progress was slow and the further objectives for the attacking troops were not achieved because of stiff resistance. As the British artillery reduced, the Australian infantry fell back under the pressure of counter-attacks launched from all sides. As the survivors withdrew, 'through an inferno of machine-gun fire', they left

Front line positions at Oppy during the British offensive in April.

behind many men who became POWs. By early afternoon it was all over; 4 Australian Brigade had been almost destroyed against a loss of just 750 men.

Further east, the French were about to become involved but, fortunately for the defenders, new fortifications were under way in the shape of the Hunding Stellung and the Brunhild Stellung, with considerable further work being done to turn a slender fortified zone into an exceptionally strong one. 'Fresh divisions were brought in, from the "pool" created by the withdrawal; the heavy artillery was reinforced; large reserves of munitions were amassed. The Crown Prince established at Sedan a Senior Officers' School – similar to that of *Prince Rupprecht's Army Group* at Valenciennes – for instruction in the new principles of the "Abwehrschlacht", or defensive battle. Some training of the troops was also possible, and the pause afforded by the withdrawal' notably improved morale. There were 21 divisions in the front line, with 17 in reserve against 53 French divisions.

Due to bad weather conditions, the French attack was postponed until 16 April for the G.A.R., and for the G.A.C. to the following day. 'On many parts of the front, however, it appeared that the breaches made in the wire defences were not complete or had been repaired, and it was evident to the most optimistic that the infantry had a heavy task before it'.

The morning started misty with an overclouded sky and, almost from the start, it was evident that the preparation had been incomplete. Under an often light counter-barrage, the French troops advanced into heavy machine gun fire; there were many casualties and, where any success was gained, the French positions soon met with counter-attacks. Later in the day, French troops in the bigger penetrations faced full-scale counter-attacks which French tanks pushed forward and helped beat off. But in most cases the infantry were too exhausted to keep up. Tank losses were high, particularly to the west of the Miette river, where the French tanks were observed leaving the Bois de Beau Marais bombarded by artillery, with twenty-three being destroyed before they reached the front line.

On the Chemin des Dames ridge, even less progress was made by the French, and all that remained in French control by evening was the support line, two or three hundred yards behind the front. The French 'losses had been very heavy and hardly a division was capable of another serious effort. Where the attack had been most successful, it was still short of the line which it was to have reached by 9.30 a.m. On the other hand, a very large haul of prisoners, over 7,000, had been captured'. The story was the same all along the attack front and the breakthrough promised to the French troops had not been achieved, although there was success the next day when the French Sixth Army continued its attacks and, by keeping up steady pressure, forced the voluntary abandonment of the defence triangle Braye–Conde–Laffaux, where many guns (some undamaged) and large amounts of munitions were left behind. Although the maximum advance by 20 April was only four miles, the French had taken 20,000 prisoners and 147 guns, freed the railway from Soissons to Reims, taken the Aisne valley west of the Oise–Aisne Canal and the second position south of Juvincourt, along with some of the most important peaks in Champagne. However, resolute defence had made the French losses very heavy – over 96,000 by 25 April, and, although the loss of defending troops was less, it was still very high at over 83,000. The German High Command claimed it as a victory because the French had not broken through, but the fighting men on both sides knew it was a victory for no one. In French political circles, any success there had been was nullified by a disappointment that turned it into a failure, looked upon with anger, disillusionment and horror; heads had to roll and a number of Generals were replaced, including Nivelle.

Even so, the French offensive was continued for a considerable time with some large scale attacks producing only a very limited amount of success, including the capture of the Californie plateau, and the capture of the Hindenburg Line on a two and a half mile front on the Chemin des Dames ridge, advances that bit deeply into the salient opposite Laffaux. The total losses to the French up to 10 May were approximately 28,500 prisoners and 187 guns.

The failure of the Nivelle offensive had a further effect towards the end of May: mutiny. Unfortunately the High Command did not believe the reports of a French troop mutiny until it was too late to use the information. And while the French offensive continued, the British had to continue to support its ally by continuing the Arras battle, knowing that there was no real chance of repeating the success of 9 April.

The battle was not all one-sided. In an attempt to aid the Arras Front, General von Moser was given approval for a four-division attack at Lagnicourt in the Amiens – Cambrai sector. The attack, which was hurriedly planned, 'had as its objectives the destruction of the greatest possible number of guns and the mauling of the defence to such an extent that it would be unable to mount an operation against the Siegfried Line for some time to come.'

Luck was not with the troops; at 0405 hours the attacking troops were met by rapid rifle and Lewis gun fire from Australian troops that successfully checked any advance. When rockets were used to illuminate the Australian positions they also lit up the advancing troops who were mown down and forced back in disorder. Although initially successful in other areas of the attack, increasing Australian resistance slowed down the advance and eventually held it, except directly in front of Lagnicourt. Here the Australian positions were attacked in overwhelming strength, without a preliminary bombardment, and successfully broken, allowing the troops to enter the village. The retreating Australians left behind four artillery batteries in Lagnicourt and a further three batteries to the west – in total twenty-two guns were captured and wired for destruction, but only five were actually destroyed before they were recaptured by the Australians. However, this success had created a small salient with Australians on three sides and, when they counter-attacked, any hope of a further advance was quelled. The troops' resistance collapsed as they made for their original starting lines, many being killed by artillery as they tried to retreat through their own wire.

The attack was carried out by *2 Guard Reserve, 3 Guard, 38 Division*, and *4 Ersatz Division*, with 21 battalions in the first line. Each division was followed by two or three batteries for close support, and by parties of engineers to effect demolitions. There were hitches due to lack of preparation and knowledge of the ground, the chief result of which was that several units were very late. Little of any real significance was achieved by the attack, except by *2 Guard Reserve Division* and the *Lehr Regiment* of *3 Guard Division* on its left, who took Lagnicourt at the cost of 800 men. The total casualty list for the attack was 2,313, including four officers and 358 other ranks taken prisoner.

The divisions facing the British attack on 23 April had not changed since being relieved on 14 April. The only division that had been there at the opening of the battle was *220 Division,* and it was not engaged until the British approached the

Sensée brook. There had been slight adjustments to the troop positions, with 26 Division now being south of the Scarpe instead of astride it.

'220 Division lay astride the Sensée and from about the Héninel-Croisilles road, was 35 Division, with its right flank on the Cojeul river. From the Cojeul to the northern edge of the Bois du Sart was 3 Bavarian and down to the Scarpe was 26 Division. From the Scarpe – the boundary between the two Corps, Gruppe Arras and Gruppe Vimy – to the southern outskirts of Gavrelle, was 18 Division, and from Gavrelle to Oppy was 17 Division. In immediate reserve from south to north were the 199, 221, 185, and 208 Divisions. 9 Grenadier Regiment, part of 3 Guard Division that was in line near Bullecourt, had been detached and was held in reserve to Group Arras.'

'On the extreme British right 220 Division ejected the 1/Queen's from its lodgement in the Hindenburg Line, but met with tough resistance.' The three regiments of 35 Division (each approximately a British brigade) were each, more or less, facing a British division. 176 Regiment was driven out of the Seigfried line, but retook it by a dramatic counter-attack. 61 Regiment repulsed the frontal attack of 30 British Division. However, the front battalion of 141 Regiment was not as fortunate and it was overrun by the British 50 Division, but its support battalion restored the situation. The regiment was finally over-whelmed by the evening attack of the British 50 Division. 35 Division was not reinforced, and was withdrawn at night through 199 Division, which was placed in the Chérisy-Riegel. 35 Division had suffered heavily, with 141 Regiment alone losing 1,089 officers and men, upwards of two-thirds of its fighting strength, and 19 machine guns.

The failure of the British attacks north and south of the Souchez river was due primarily to the fact that they came up against the new system of defence, for which no provision had been made. Four regiments were involved in the defence: 35 Regiment on Hill 65, and 118 Regiment of 56 Division, and 34 and 266 Reserve Regiments, with its left on the Lens-Vimy railway, both from 80 Reserve Division. They repulsed the attacks without reinforcements, so that the counter-attack division, 1 Guard Reserve, behind this sector of Gruppe Souchez, could be sent that same evening southwards to assist Gruppe Vimy in its effort to recapture the lost ground at Gavrelle.

On the British VI Corps front, three divisions, 15, 17, and 29, were opposed by two divisions, 3 Bavarian and 26 Infantry. 'The former had a bad day on its right flank, where 18 Bavarian Regiment lost Guémappe and suffered 808 casualties.' 9 Grenadier Regiment, put in to counter-attack north of the Cambrai road, recovered some ground, and on its right beat off the renewed attacks of 29 British Division. The whole division and the Grenadiers who had supported it were relieved on the night of 24 April by 221 Division.

British Intelligence kept detailed records of all the divisions that they fought against; in their view *26 Division* was not only one of the hardest fighting in the Army but also alert and well led. Realising that Lone Copse valley afforded the British a good assembly position, *125 Regiment* established a concealed outpost at a point where it could look down into the depression. It reported the assembly of the British *17 Division's* troops half an hour before the assault, with disastrous consequences for them. As well as losing hardly any ground, *26 Division* was able to hold its own front and assist the counter-attack on Roeux.

North of the Scarpe, *86 Regiment* on the left of *18 Division* had just been relieved by *161 Regiment* of *185 Division*, the local counter-attack division. Driven out of Roeux by 51 British Division, *161 Regiment* had recently retaken the place by a counter-attack. *86 Regiment* was then thrown in, but failed to recapture Roeux Station and the Chemical Works. However, by 0900 hours this important position had been taken by a battalion of *65 Regiment* (*208 Division*). The other two regiments of *18 Division* (*31* and *85*) were so severely mauled that another regiment, *89 Grenadier*, belonging to *17 Division* but held in corps reserve was brought up north of the railway, but failed to recover the line of the Roeux–Gavrelle road. *18 Division* and all troops which had been attached to it were relieved on 24 April by *208 Division*.

Only *90 Regiment*, on the left of *17 Division,* was involved in the morning assault. The battalion in the Oppy line was destroyed by the British 63 (Royal Naval) Division, 'and the defence of Gavrelle then depended on a company in a quarry on the eastern side, which never readied its battle station. Fusilier Lutmer was in Gavrelle when the 'Sea Soldiers' attacked. 'Due to the large bombardment we had hidden in the cellar of a large house. Sergeant Kloke shouted, "Tommies are here!" so we took up position by the shattered windows on the ground floor. Before we got a chance to open fire, a Tommy threw a grenade into the room which bounced along the floorboards.' Luck was with them when the sergeant managed to pick up and return it to its owner before it exploded. They then started to fire again but, being on the ground floor, were easy targets; Lutmer saw two of his school chums shot through the head. Quickly they were surrounded and realized that further resistance was pointless. Then his luck ran out: 'another grenade was thrown into the room and Kloke picked it up to throw back but this time he was too late; it exploded in his hand. There was a terrific bang and then whistling in the ears and the next thing I know, I woke up in the street outside the house where I had been dragged. I had many shrapnel wounds from the British bomb…everyone else had been killed by the bomb.' He was then taken to hospital.

'The *Reserve Battalion* was ordered to rally the troops which had been driven back and retake Gavrelle, but its counter-attack broke down completely.' The next to attack was *185 Division*, the local counter-attack division. Two battalions of *28 Reserve Regiment* advanced across the open from the direction of Izel under heavy artillery fire, but they were stopped by the infantry of 37 and 63 British Divisions on the outskirts of Gavrelle. Further attempts next morning were also decisively defeated.

Gruppe Vimy, however, knew that the Gavrelle positions were too important not to recover. It now had at its disposal *1 Guard Division*, formerly the counter-attack division to *Gruppe Souchez*, further north. This division was sent down when it was discovered that the attack on La Coulotte was not serious. In the afternoon, *64 Reserve Regiment* of *1 Guard Division* was put in to make a counter-attack from Mauville Farm. 'The regimental commander was given control of all troops already in front of Gavrelle, with orders to carry them forward with his fresh battalions. The result was another costly failure. It is clear from regimental accounts, that though the British barrages caused heavy loss, it was in the last

Captured troops being used to take Canadian wounded back to a field dressing station.

resort the machine guns of the defence that defeated the counter-attacks.' *64 Reserve Regiment* then relieved the shattered remnants of *28* and *90 Reserve Regiments* in front of Gavrelle. More successfully, to the north a number of British POWs were taken when a machine gun company fired into their attack.

As the battle was beginning to die down, unknown to the defenders, the British were getting ready to attack again. On 28 April there was to be a further attempt to capture Oppy and Arleux, to the north Fresnes-les-Montauban, Neuvireuil, Fresnoy and Acheville were to be attacked, while, in the southern sector of the Arras front, fresh assaults were planned against Greenland Hill, Roeux, Fontaine lez Croisilles, Chérisy, Vis en Artois, Boiry Notre Dame, Plouvain and Bullecourt. If these assaults succeeded, troops garrisoning the Siegfried Line between Banteux and Havrincourt would be the next to be attacked.

To the north of Arras, British shells cut the wire, while to the south the British artillery preparation included counter battery fire for destruction, harassing fire by night, and bombardment with gas shell. The important sidings at Brebières were shelled by 9.2 and 12 inch railway guns to put them out of action. On 27 April,

British trenches to the south of Arras were persistently shelled, with particular attention being paid to the Monchy-Pelves road at 2100 hours the same evening; the target was the junction of two British divisions. The bombardment was followed by a strong attack aimed at recovering the front line lost on 24 April. The assault was carried out by three battalions, two from *26 Division* and one from *221 Division*, but was repulsed although some ground was reoccupied, no British positions were taken.

28 April was a bright, mild day but the visibility was poor. 'From the Scarpe to about 1,000 yards south of Gavrelle the *208th Division* had four regiments in line, from left to right *65th* (detached from *185th Division* and the only regiment of that division not used up in the Second Battle of the Scarpe), *65th Reserve, 185th*, and *25th*, the two first approximately opposed to the British 34th Division and the other two to the 37th.'

The 34 Division attack passed right through Roeux, but left a few men holding out in the village. The British then pressed on to the high ground above Plouvain, where 400 "English and Scottish troops" established themselves. These survivors beat off the first counter-attack, but the reserve battalion of the *65th Regiment* was then brought up to attack them from the south. Almost surrounded, the greater part of the British were captured. Roeux was then counter-attacked and regained, with the troops getting a footing in the old British line. From this, however, they were speedily ejected.

The history of *25 Regiment* (on the right of the attack) states 'that a British battalion with machine guns was seen advancing along the Gavrelle–Fresnes road, north of the regimental sector. The machine-gun company of the right battalion took this column and its line of retreat under such effective fire that it surrendered in a body to the division on the right.' However, while British records agree that the 2/R. Marines did lose a very large number of prisoners, they show that the whole battalion did not surrender. 'Meanwhile part of the British 37th Division had broken clean through, driven the three battalion staffs out of Hollow Copse, only narrowly been stopped from entering the rear line of defence west of Fresnes and beaten off a counter-attack by the reserve battalion. At midday a battalion of the *1st Guard Reserve Division*, from the sector on the right, attacked this detachment from north and north-west; the battalion of the 25th renewed its attack simultaneously ; and the British were overwhelmed, losing 125 prisoners.'

64 Reserve Regiment was the only regiment of *1 Guard Reserve Division* in the line; on its right was *75 Regiment* of *17 Division*, that had not been engaged on 23 April. The right battalion of *64 Reserve*, north of the Gavrelle–Fresnes road, was almost destroyed by the British 63 Division's attack. However, a counter-attack by a battalion of *2 Guard Reserve Regiment* restored the situation; the battalion retook the windmill; but this was in British hands at the end of the day. On the right, only one battalion of *75 Regiment* held a front of a thousand yards, from just north of the railway to north of Oppy. To stabilize the front, the support and reserve battalions were thrown in to counter-attack, and by about noon had regained their regimental sector, though only after fierce fighting with parties of the British 2 Division.

North of Oppy up to Acheville was *111 Division*, which had two battalions – on the right one from *76 Regiment* and on the left one from *73 Regiment* – in the forward trench of the Arleux Loop (as it was known to the British), or 'Nose', to the defending troops). The Canadians broke through the 'Nose' in the sector of *73 Regiment*, 'attacked from the rear and captured the companies still holding out, rolled up the battalion of the 76th from the flank thus opened, and captured the western side' of the 'Nose' and the village of Arleux. Although this was an important position to hold, it was not vital as long as the Fresnoy Line in the rear was held, so the divisional commander forbade a counter-attack. The front line battalion of *73 Regiment* had 400 men missing.

By the end of the April battles, the Oppy Line was in British hands to within two hundred yards of the wood. The fighting in this area had been fierce and stubborn, with both sides fighting with bravery and determination. From both sides the volume of artillery fire had been tremendous, with the German fire being particularly accurate and effective, especially on the attack front of 99 British Brigade prior to their attack on 29 April, when most of the stored small arms ammunition, grenades and water were destroyed.

On 29 April, Admiral Müller recorded 'good news from the Arras front. The English attacks have been beaten off with bloody losses.' And two days later he wrote: 'In bitter fighting our troops at Arras have withstood the attacks of the English, who are believed to have suffered very heavy losses'. However, 'our losses were also stressed, particularly our loss of commissioned ranks.'

The casualty figures for April show just how heavy the fighting was – over 78,000 officers and men. 'The sick wastage for the month numbered 1,896 officers and 49,260 other ranks. These latter figures comprise little over two and a half per cent of a force numbering, with labour units, 1,910,400.' The loss during April to the three British Armies 'engaged in the offensive, including perhaps 800 prisoners taken in the final operations against the outpost villages, were 17,959 prisoners and 254 guns; 11,295 prisoners and 185 guns by the British Third Army, 5,784 prisoners and 69 guns by the British First, and 880 prisoners by the British Fifth Army. This total of just on 18,000 prisoners in a month may be compared with the 39,000 prisoners taken by the British in the twenty weeks of the Battles of the Somme'.

And so the battle continued with the 3rd Battle of the Scarpe. Attack was met with counter-attack and loss of life on both sides. Although the British attacks pushed

28cm railway gun on the Arras front.

their line forward, nowhere was it conclusive, and the main structures of the Siegfried Stellung were still in place – or, if they had been dented, were replaced by new lines behind them; importantly a lynchpin – the Oppy sector – was secure, however hard the fighting to take it.

According to the British *Official History* 'the British failure was in general so complete that the defence was able to repulse the attack or drive out troops which had broken into its positions without calling upon divisions in reserve. The impression left by the accounts in regimental histories emphasizes the British infantry's lack of power of resistance when counter-attacked by quite small bodies of troops'.

The British plan of attack was flawed and allowed the defenders to reap a rich harvest. To their advantage, the sun did not rise until 0522 hours, and the moon was not only nearly full, but did not set until sixteen minutes before the British attack began. This provided a clear view of the impending attack. 'On large stretches of the front the troops assembling…were silhouetted against its light as it sank behind them, their appearance giving warning of the attack and drawing heavy fire.' The British *Official History* summarized the major problems of the attack as: 'the confusion caused by the darkness; the speed with which the German artillery opened fire; the manner in which it concentrated upon the British infantry, almost neglecting the artillery; the intensity of its fire, the heaviest that many an experienced (British) soldier had ever witnessed, seemingly unchecked by British counter-battery fire and lasting almost without slackening for fifteen hours; the readiness with which the German infantry yielded to the first assault and the energy of its counter-attack;' and agreeing with German Regimental histories that the British troops were unable to withstand any resolute counter-attack.

Although bombarded by British artillery, not all positions had been affected; Tool Trench, in the front line, lay just behind a crest and had suffered little. Its garrison stood shoulder to shoulder to meet the British attack, and such was the strength of its fire power that the attack was smashed. Any troops that fought their way into the position were taken prisoner. In other sectors, the British troops were fired upon from defenders who had pushed forward into the shell holes of no-man's-land and had thus not been affected by the barrage that had fallen behind them. Some attacking battalions moved forward but, when the flank battalions were checked and pushed back, their positions became untenable and they were also forced to move back by counter-attacks.

Artillery fire also caused considerable casualties when the British front line was deluged, just before the attack, with chemical and high explosive shell. At zero, the British field batteries were enveloped in thick clouds of gas. As well as causing casualties and confusion among the attacking troops, it also caused casualties amongst the reserve troops; the severity of the barrage is clearly shown by two battalions suffering 350 casualties just going up to the British front line.

Again the attacks against Roeux, Greenland Hill and the Chemical Works faltered but even the use of heavy howitzers could not dislodge the defenders, and as in other sectors the darkness caused hopeless confusion amongst the British attackers. Being familiar with their environment gave the defenders a considerable advantage in the darkness, allowing them to hide until the last minute. Hiding behind a wall facing the British Household Battalion was a machine gun that opened up as the line of soldiers came level with it, to terrible effect. The darkness did not allow quick identification of the troops in the immediate area. One battalion walked into a defended position, thinking they were following their sister battalion, to heavy loss while men of one battalion, having wheeled too far right, attacked their own trenches in confusion, firing at the position from the hip.

The front was held, during this phase of the battle by seven divisions, some of whom were fresh, whereas only two of the eleven British divisions were new to the battle. *49 Reserve Division* on the left, from the Sensée to southeast of Chérisy, had just arrived from Flanders; *199 Division* newly arrived from the south garrisoned positions between Chérisy and Cojeul river; *221 Division*, from the Cojeul river to the Bois des Aubépines, had previously been in action on 23 April; the next division north to the Scarpe, *9 Reserve Division*, arrived on the night of 29 April. *208 Division*, in position from the Scarpe to the southeast of Gavrelle, had previously been heavily involved in the fighting; to such an extent that its exhausted *25 Regiment* had been replaced by a fresh regiment, *17 Bavarian Reserve* from *6 Bavarian Reserve Division*. Holding the important sector, southeast of Gavrelle to the Oppy-Bailleul road, was *1 Guard Reserve* (a counter-attack unit), a division that had had all its regiments heavily involved in the fighting. Attached to this division and holding the centre sector, was *185 Division*, another unit that had suffered heavily; holding the final sector between the Oppy-Bailleul road and halfway between Fresnoy and Acheville, was *15 Reserve Division*, a completely fresh division.

The defending troops were able to repulse the attack and drive the British troops, who had broken into their positions without using any divisions in reserve. Between the Sensée and the Cojeul, on the front held by *49 Reserve* and *199 Divisions*, 'where the British had great initial success, it took only three platoons to retake Chérisy', emphasising the British lack of resistance to even weak counter-attacks during this phase of operations.

'Some of the hardest fighting was immediately north of the Cojeul, where the 169th Brigade of the 56th Division broke through the *41st Regiment, 221st Division*. Part of this attack swung northwards across the Cambrai road, and took the front line further north, but was, in its turn, mopped up by the…reserve battalion.' In the zone of attack for the British 167 Brigade, the artillery fire completely missed the frontline held by *60 Reserve Regiment* (*221 Division*) allowing the defenders to stand up and fire into the attacking masses, annihilating the leading waves. Many prisoners were taken and little ground was lost, with only *9 Reserve Division* losing any ground permanently.

The British 4 Division broke through north of the Scarpe on the front held by *65* and *185 Regiments* of *208 Division*. 'The regimental reserves, aided by the *25th Regiment,* in divisional reserve, restored the situation.' The *British Official History* records what it achieved as 'a wonderful feat. Counter-attacking up the Scarpe valley, with its left on the river, its right company came unexpectedly upon a body of British troops, from which it captured 150 prisoners and three machine guns. A second party of British troops was then encountered, from which, with the aid of a detachment of the *185th Regiment,* it took fifty more prisoners. Yet another party was then overrun, so that, by the time it had re-entered Roeux and rescued a pioneer company still holding out there, it had in its hands 358 prisoners. Its own losses are given as 117. It must be added, however, that this regiment had a casualty list of just under one thousand between the 23rd April and the 3rd May.' Several other regiments suffered similar losses. The heaviest losses were at Fresnoy; here many defenders were taken prisoner and the counter-attacks were unsuccessful. *17 Reserve Regiment* (*15 Reserve Division*) alone reported 650 casualties. British casualties were also high and some of the fighting was reminiscent of 1 July 1916.

'The *5th Bavarian Division*, assembling about Douai between the 1st and 3rd May, received orders on the 5th to recapture Fresnoy. The operation was to be a deliberate counter-attack (Gegenangriff, as opposed to the Gegenstoss or immediate counter-attack, frequently carried out in the course of the battle). All three regiments were put in, the *21st* with its right on the Lille road, along which ran the northern edge of Fresnoy Park ; the *19th* thence to the southern edge of the wood south of Fresnoy; and the *7th* against the remainder of the British position in the salient. The attack was supported by 27 field and 17 heavy batteries, not taking into account the artillery of neighbouring divisions.'

21 Regiment reported only one temporary hold-up. 'After that the battlefield was empty except for dead and abandoned arms and equipment. The strongest resistance came from the edge of Fresnoy Park, on the regiment's left flank, but it was speedily stifled. The *19th* in the centre lost the barrage owing to heavy rain having turned the ground to the consistency of glue. It also met with stronger resistance from the British and might not have reached its objective had not the *21st* disengaged its right. The *7th* also had trouble, but bombed up the trench south of the wood, rolling up the British front —that is, the line of the 1/East Surrey.'

'This highly successful attack was carried out in depth, each regiment having two battalions in line and one in reserve, and each battalion two companies in line, one in support, and one in reserve. The company passing through Fresnoy village was provided with a Flammenwerfer. The leading waves were ordered to push straight through to the final objective; the supports to clear the captured ground and provide flank protection; and the reserves to fill gaps or cooperate in neighbouring sectors. The losses were comparatively heavy, 1,585 for the infantry alone, which probably means 1,750 in all.'

The successful defence of Bullecourt against an Australian attack on 11 April resulted in the British Fifth Army preparing a renewed attack. From 12 April, an increasing amount of artillery bombarded the approaches to the village, reducing troop movements, cutting the wire and smashing artillery positions. The last remaining houses were demolished, but the rubble fell as cover for the deep cellars, providing extra protection as did the remains of the walls. The second attempt to take Bullecourt started at 0345 hours on 3 May and after twenty-four hours fighting, the defences had held, except opposite the Australian 6 Brigade; even here it did not look like a permanent loss.

Zerstörter engl. Tank vor Arras

Mark II training tank captured on 11 April near Arras.

At the end of four days' fighting, the strong defence had used up two attacking British divisions and caused serious casualties to two more. This had only been achieved by slightly adjusting the front, using large numbers of troops in defence as well as in the half dozen counter-attacks, and by bringing reserves. The British attack was developing into a slow and ferocious struggle in which success was measured by the yard, and, as Bullecourt was still untaken, it left the attackers with two options: abandon any territory taken, or continue sending brigade after brigade into the fight.

On 11 May, the defensive positions at Roeux were overrun by British troops. Five days later, a counter-attack was carried out by fresh troops – *38 Division* that had come from the Quéant area and had been in reserve to the *Sixth Army* for a week. 'The operation was entitled "Erfurt", the use of such a code-name always implying that the German command meant business; again it was a Gegenangriff in the fullest sense. The *94th Regiment* attacked the station and the Chemical Works, the *95th* the village of Roeux.'

'Some companies came under hot fire on their way up and were delayed, but they just managed to assault in time, behind the barrage. The attack of the *95th* was, generally speaking, a failure. That of the *94th* was almost completely successful, but the battalions had suffered so heavily that they could not resist the British counter-attacks especially as the British artillery and machine guns prevented their reinforcement. Finally, except for one company which held on north of the railway, the survivors withdrew to their starting-line.' *94 Regiment* suffered 547 casualties - those of *95 Regiment* are unknown. 'It was as complete a failure as the counter-attack on Fresnoy had been a success. On 20 May *49 Reserve Division* was attacked by the British 33 Division with the main thrust falling on the centre regiment – *225 Reserve*. The regiment held an awkward sector that formed a salient; 'on the right the Cherisy-Riegel from the Fontaine—Heninel road to the Hindenburg Line, and on the left the Hindenburg Line to a distance of 1,000 yards south-east of the Sensée. On both sides of the angle the defence collapsed with heavy casualties, and the regiment was severely shaken. On the 21st May the division was relieved by the *220th* which had previously held this front and which faced the later attack of the 33rd Division.'

By 13 May, apart from an area known as the 'Red Patch', the whole of Bullecourt was now in British hands. Attacks that day were held by the defenders, as were those the next day. During the night an intense bombardment caused heavy casualties among the British, destroying much of their positions in the Hindenburg line. In the morning the artillery was joined by trench mortar fire that levelled the trenches with their big projectiles. British field artillery units were enveloped in gas, as were the counter batteries, but they managed to put down a protective barrage. 'The flashes of explosions, the fantastic firework display as rockets of all colours were flung up, calling, it might be, for aid, for fire to lengthen, or fire to shorten – no observer could in the confusion recognize signals or even tell whose were the rockets – made a truly awful and infernal battle picture, to which the din was fitting accompaniment.'

A little before 0400 hours on 15 May, the Australian and British troops faced the last and biggest counter-attack at Bullecourt. It extended over the whole front and was designed to recapture it in its entirety. Only in Bullecourt did the counter-attack meet with any success; in other places the frontal assault was smashed or, where successful, was quickly routed. After a prolonged and fluctuating struggle in the village, a British counter-attack pushed the attackers back. By the end of the day, Bullecourt had been lost, but the official communiqué stated that it had evacuated in accordance with orders.

'For fourteen days some of the most savage fighting of the war had taken place around the ruins of a small village and over a stretch of ground slightly under a mile of width'. Casualties were heavy: 'by the end the dead of both sides lay in clumps all over the battlefield, and in the bottom or under the parapets of trenches many hundreds had been hastily covered with a little earth.' The British losses were extremely heavy at over 14,000 or 1000 a day; losses among the defenders were also heavy but not at the level of their attackers', with *3 Guard Division* recording losses of over 2,000 and *27 Division* reporting over 2,300 in the infantry alone; the losses of the other six regiments involved are unknown.

Although this was officially the end of the battle for the British, local encounters continued for many days in order to show that the battle of Arras had not finished. 'It was not the sole operation fought for this purpose; for before it had ended another attack had been launched against the Chemical Works at Roeux, and, after it was over, further attempts were made against the Hindenburg Line near Bullecourt.'

While the Bullecourt attacks were taking place, a further assault was launched against the Chemical Works and the nearby château and cemetery. As with previous attempts, any success was limited and was mainly attributable to the quality of the defending troops opposing 4 British Division. Their attack had fallen mainly on *4 Ersatz Division,* a 'luckless formation, from the Havrincourt area (that) had failed in the Lagnicourt counter-offensive, had been harassed and harried by the left wing of the Fourth Army when closing up to the Hindenburg Line, and had now been transferred to the wasps' nest of Roeux.' Its losses were large with over 450 taken as prisoners. *6 Bavarian Reserve Division* to the north, a division of stouter troops, resisted the attack.

Throughout 15 May, British positions were bombarded prior to an attempt to recover the lost ground. At 0345 hours the next day, the troops advanced behind a heavy barrage. After heavy fighting some positions were retaken and held, but not the important Chemical Works. However, British attempts to take Infantry Hill on 19 May were stopped and some prisoners taken. A further British attack on 30 May at 2330 hours was spotted as troops left their trenches fifteen minutes before zero hour and, within five minutes, the requested artillery barrage was sufficiently powerful to break the attack. Any groups that penetrated the front line were surrounded the next day and forced to surrender.

The battles around Arras from now on would be small operations that did not require large numbers of troops or artillery. British reinforcements would henceforth go to those divisions scheduled for the next big attacks to the north in Flanders, and artillery units would be slowly withdrawn to assist future offensives.

Although the battle of Arras was over for the British by the end of the month, there were other operations in June, and a successful attack against Hill 70 in mid-August by Canadian troops. In this assault, the defenders were driven back and the hill occupied by Canadian troops who were able to advance no further. Local

The lucky ones from the Allied offensives found themselves as prisoners in France well away from the war.

counter-attacks in the early morning to retake the hill were broken up by artillery fire, while, later in the morning, the massed infantry in extended order were caught in artillery barrage of field and heavy artillery that was vividly described, after the war in the regimental histories: 'they marched across the open through fountains of earth sent up by the heavy shells, and later through a hail of shrapnel and machine gun bullets.' In all, the Canadians repulsed eighteen counter-attacks and, the next day, when they continued their attacks, came across troops massing for a counter-attack. After fierce close fighting, the counter-attack troops withdrew, leaving behind one hundred dead, an equal number of wounded, and thirty prisoners. Counter-attacks later in the day, lasting around ninety minutes, similarly failed to dislodge the Canadians. Hill 70 was a vital observation area and the attacks and counter-attacks lasted for six days, with the Canadians eventually holding the hill and moving down towards Cité St. Emile. Fighting continued until the end of the month with no change in the situation. A further British assault was planned for 15 October to take Lens and the high ground around Sallaumines, but a lack of troops, due to the Flanders offensive, meant it could not take place.

The major French offensive, at the same time as the British Arras offensive, had been a failure with numerous mutinies; the French Army was no longer fit for offensive fighting. Although the French troops were prepared to defend their lines, they would not attack. As a result of the unreliability of the French Army during this period, the British offensive at Arras had to continue in order to conceal this problem, and, when Arras finally did finish, the focus would move to the Flanders plain and a further British offensive – Third Ypres. The British *Official History* recorded that 'the campaign was fought by Sir Douglas Haig, on a front favourable on account of its strategic advantages, in order to prevent the Germans falling upon the French Armies, shaken and dispirited after three years of unceasing warfare and finally mutinous in consequence of the losses in and failure of the Nivelle offensive, upon which such great hopes had been set'. However, OHL received information from a spy that there would be an attack in the Ypres area so that there would be no surprise when it came. This was further corroborated by information from prisoners taken on the Arras front; 'statements of prisoners proved conclusively that no further big attacks were to be expected in the Arras sector, and that a big attack was to take place from the Armentieres-Ypres front about the 7th June, after an eight-day bombardment'.

After two months of intensive fighting, the Arras Front would now become a comparatively quiet front as both belligerents focused their attentions on the Ypres Salient. It would be nearly a year before Arras became an important area again, and then only for a very short while.

Lessons had been learned from the Arras offensive that were applied to the French offensive and later: very importantly the need to supply reserves with speed when and where they were needed, and the principle of a fluid defence that kept the men away from the immediate front line whenever possible. This Abwehrschlacht gave a new sense of confidence. 'The infantry, observing the rhythmic flow of the reserves in each engagement, gained an impression of leadership as something vital, active, and ever watchful of their fortunes. No unit henceforth felt that it was to be left to its own resources; each one knew that the machinery for supporting it existed and would be put in motion if that were humanly possible. It realized, too, that the better it fulfilled its allocated role the more efficiently would that machinery function.' It is probably this that prevented the army from crumbling under the Entente attacks of 1917, as many of their leaders feared it would.

Counter-attacks were handled well and the junior leadership was good, with the under-officer frequently showing initiative by daring and resourceful local assaults to recapture positions of importance without the aid of an officer. On the other hand, British troops who lost their officer were apt to fall back. The army had learned a great deal. Casualties had been high but not as high as among the British troops and, while some important positions had been taken, the actual ground lost was relatively small.

At dinner on 31 May, to general surprise, the Kaiser suddenly rose to his feet and said: 'General Ludendorff has just reported to me that the spring offensive at Arras, on the Aisne, and in Champagne has been defeated. We have gained a famous victory.'

Fighting around Arras, at least for the next few months, would be localised attacks and trench raids of specific tactical necessity. Troop numbers would be deliberately kept at a minimum to allow a maximum input into the defence of Flanders and, at the end of the year, at Cambrai. There would be little change until well into 1918.

After the battle around Ypres and then at Cambrai, the army had started to change and manpower became a serious issue. 'In millions of letters from the Western Front from April to November came the ever-rising bitter complaints of the almost unbearable hardships and bloody losses in the scarcely interrupted chain of battles: Arras, Aisne-Champagne (Nivelle), Flanders, Verdun and the Chemin des Dames (Malmaison). A hundred thousand leave men told the Home Front by word of mouth the details of the ever-growing superiority of the enemy, particularly in weapons of destruction.' So, by the end of 1917, after the Flanders battle – 'the greatest martyrdom of the World War' – had consumed the German strength to such a degree that the harm done could no longer be repaired, 'the sharp edge of the German sword had become jagged.' However, the German Army was still a most formidable force and was being reinforced by first class troops from the Eastern Front.

What was not realised at the time was how much the army's will to carry on the struggle was being eroded. Troops from Russia did not all welcome the transfer. Many who had witnessed a successful end to the campaign had hoped that their fighting days were now over and had no wish to join their comrades in the bloodbath in the west. There were many troops who disappeared during the transfer from one front to another. The railway trucks transporting the men were often painted with appropriate slogans that expressed their feelings: Schlachtvieh für Flandern – fattened beasts for Flanders or beasts to be slaughtered for Flanders. As the trains moved across Germany, societies established to help men who were prepared to desert did just that, and many men simply vanished from the army. This movement was particularly active in the major cities across the country. It is estimated that up to ten per cent of the troops moving west were provided with forged papers, money and ration cards, and helped to cross into Holland and Switzerland.

Further numbers of troops were to come from the released prisoners of war. However, many of them had become socialists during their time in captivity and

Christliches Andenken im Gebete
an den tugendsamen Jüngling

Josef Linner

Rauschhuber-Bauerssohn v. Rauschwaltham, Pfarrvikariat Waldhausen
Gefr. b. 2. Res.-Inf.-Regt., 1. M.-G..K.
Inhaber des bayer. Militär-Verdienstkreuzes 3. Kl.
welcher am 9. April 1917 nach 2jähr. treuer
Pflichterfüllung infolge schwerer Verwundung
in der Schlacht bei Arras im 26. Lebensjahre
für's Vaterland den Heldentod erlitt.

Was weint Ihr, Muter, Geschwister, meine Lieben,
Weil ich nicht länger bin bei Euch geblieben?
Für Euch, fürs Vaterland bin ich gestorben,
Hab' mir den Himmel jetzt erworben.
Mit reiner Marterpalme steh ich vor Gottes Thron,
Der reich bedachte mich mit dem ewigen Lohn.
Denkt oft an mich und seid nicht bang,
Auch Euer Leben währt nicht lang.
Wie bald, wie schnell vergeht die Zeit,
Ihr seid bei mir, ich bin bei Euch,
                    dort in der Ewigkeit.

Süßes Herz Mariä sei meine Liebe! 300 Tg. Abl.
Mein Jesus Barmherzigkeit!   100 Tage Ablaß.
Süßes Herz Jesu erbarme dich d. sterbenden Krieger!

Th. Hartig, Kraiburg a. Inn.

Gefreiter Josef Linner, a farmer's son, who had won the Bavarian Military Service Cross 3rd class, was killed on 9 April 1917 while serving with 1 Machine Gun Company of 2 Bavarian Reserve Infantry Regiment.

were not reliable. For re-education they were sent to special camps but even then many were more likely to be troublemakers rather than reliable soldiers; so much so that, even during the desperate manpower shortage from summer of 1918 to the end of the war, some unit commanders would not take them, believing that they could not be trusted.

After the fighting at Ypres came the December battle of Cambrai and although little real gain had been achieved by either side, both had learned valuable lessons for the coming year: 'our action has given us valuable hints for an offensive battle in the west if we wished to undertake one in 1918' wrote Hindenburg in his memoirs and, as Rupprecht recorded, 'it was our biggest success over the British since 1915, at Ypres' and 'captures from the British, since the opening of the counter-offensive had amounted to 75 officers, 2,556 other ranks and 85 guns'. However, the enemy had taken 189 officers, 10,916 other ranks and ninety-eight guns.

Although the offensive had finished, there was continued fighting on various parts of the front; part of *16 Bavarian Division* had a limited success in a local attack on 12 December near Bullecourt and there were further successes at Messines and Polderhoek.

Apart from the fact that not all troops could be trusted to perform to their best, the advantage was now passing from Allied hands. Something needed to be done to win the war before the Americans arrived in strength. On 11 November, at Mons, the first ideas for an offensive in 1918 were discussed. General von Kuhl argued for an attack against the British at Ypres, Colonel von Schulenberg favoured an attack against the French at Verdun, but Ludendorff wanted an attack south of Ypres, with an offensive near St. Quentin offering the greatest possibilities for rolling up the British front. At a further planning conference on 27 December, Ludendorff ordered that planning and preparation should be made for attacks in a number of areas: 'George' – an offensive towards Hazebrouck with a subsidiary, 'George Two' towards Ypres, 'Michael' against St. Quentin with a subsidiary against Arras – 'Mars'. Other schemes were prepared against French positions around Verdun and in the Vosges.

Destroyed British tank near Bullecourt.

Dem Auge fern, dem Herzen ewig nah.

✝

In Gottes heiligen Frieden
ruht fern von seinen Lieben
der ehrengeachtete Herr

Kaspar Schiechtele,

Ökonom in Sachsenried,
Gefreiter beim 17. bayer. Res.-Inf.-Rgts.,
11. Kompagnie,
geboren am 6. März 1883 zu Ruderatshofen,
den Heldentod fürs Vaterland gefunden am
3. Mai 1917 bei Arras.

―――

Die Kugel, die Dich niederwarf,
Sie traf auch mich ins Herz;
Doch eines Helden Gattin darf
Nicht untergeh'n in Schmerz.
Die Kraft, die Dich im Kampf gestählt,
Sie sei mein Halt in Not;
Der Trost des Wiedersehens hält
Mich aufrecht bis zum Tod.

Barmherzigster Jesus, gib ihm die ewige Ruhe!
7 Jahr 7 Quadrag. Ablaß.
Süßes Herz Maria, sei meine Rettung!
300 Tage Ablaß.
Gelobt sei überall, das heiligste Herz Jesu!
300 Tage Ablaß.

Meiler, Druckerei, Kaufbeuren.

Twenty-nine year old Gefreiter Kaspar Schiechtele of Sachsenried, serving with *17 Bavarian Reserve Infantry Regiment*, was killed on 8 May 1917.

Daily news sheet produced by Luddendorf's headquarters on 16 April 1917 detailing how successfully the defences were holding up against British attacks, taking 475 Australian soldiers prisoner and fifteen machine guns.

1145.

16. April 1917. 4.30 Uhr nachm.

Berlin, 16. April. (Amtlich.) Großes Hauptquartier, den 16. April 1917.

Westlicher Kriegsschauplatz.

Heeresgruppe Kronprinz Rupprecht.

Auf dem Nordufer der Scarpe hielt unser Vernichtungsfeuer englische Angriffswellen nieder, sodaß der Sturm nicht zur Durchführung kam. Auch nordöstlich von Croisilles brachte unser Feuer einen starken Angriff der Engländer verlustreich zum Scheitern.

Nördlich der Straße Arras—Cambrai warf ein Vorstoß unserer Truppen den Feind auf Lagnicourt und Boursies zurück.

Zu den blutigen Verlusten der dort fechtenden Australier kommt die Einbuße von 475 Gefangenen und 15 Maschinengewehren, die eingebracht, sowie von 22 Geschützen, die genommen und durch Sprengen unbrauchbar gemacht wurden.

Bei St. Quentin nahm das Artilleriefeuer wieder zu.

Heeresgruppe Kronprinz.

Zwischen Oise und Aisne sind gestern durch starkes Feuer vorbereitete Angriffe der Franzosen bei Baugaillon und Chivres gescheitert.

Von Soissons bis Reims und im Westteil der Champagne hat der Feuerkampf bei schärfstem Einsatz der Artillerie und Minenwerfer angehalten.

Nach Scheitern feindlicher Erkundungsvorstöße am 15. April ist heute morgen in breiten Abschnitten

die Infanterie-Schlacht

entbrannt.

Armee Herzog Albrecht von Württemberg.

In der Lothringischen Ebene und der Burgundischen Pforte blieben Unternehmungen französischer Sturmtrupps gegen unsere Stellungen ohne jeden Erfolg.

N.B. Ein einheitlicher Angriff feindlicher Flieger gegen unsere Fesselballons links der Aisne war ergebnislos. Die Gegner haben zwischen Soissons und Verdun gestern elf Flugzeuge verloren, deren Mehrzahl Maschinen neuester Bauart (Spads) sind.

Östlicher Kriegsschauplatz.

Im allgemeinen geringe Gefechtstätigkeit. Nur an der Bahn Kowel-Luck verfeuerte die russische Artillerie etwa 10 000 Schuß gegen unsere Stellungen. Vordringende Streifabteilungen wurden abgewiesen.

Mazedonische Front.

Keine besonderen Ereignisse.

(W.T.B.)   Der Erste Generalquartiermeister.
                                    Ludendorff.

――――

Neue U-Bootbeute im Mittelmeer.

Berlin, 16. April. (Amtlich.) Im Mittelmeer wurden nach neu eingegangenen Meldungen versenkt: 6 Dampfer und 4 Segler mit 40 782 To., darunter am 10. April ein englischer Hilfskreuzer Typ „Ottway" von etwa 12 000 To.

Fliegerangriff auf Freiburg.

Berlin, 16. April. Am Sonnabend, den 14. April, mittags 12 Uhr griff ein feindliches Flugzeuggeschwader von 12 Flugzeugen die offene Stadt Freiburg im Breisgau an. Der Angriff wurde um 5 Uhr mit zwei anderen Geschwadern mit zusammen 23 Flugzeugen wiederholt. Von unseren Fliegern wurden zwei feindliche Flugzeuge abgeschossen und ein drittes von der Erde aus zum Absturz gebracht.

Troops in bivouac, using their waterproof cloaks to make tents, wait their turn to be called to the front at Arras.

Christliches Andenken
im Gebete
an den tugendsamen Jüngling

Anton Helsberger,

Wallnersohn in Grünwald
(Expositur Oberornau,)
**Soldat im bay. Inf.-Regt. Nr. 3
11. Komp.,**

welcher am 8. Mai 1917 infolge
eines Artillerieschusses in Ceruy
bei Arras im 20. Lebensjahre den
Heldentod fürs Vaterland starb.

Was weint ihr Eltern, Geschwister meine Lieben
Weil ich nicht länger bin bei Euch geblieben.
Es ist nicht weit blickt auf zum Stern,
Dort oben wohn' ich, garnicht fern.
Und früh geschieden? — hab't nicht bang
Auch Euer Leben ist nicht lang
Wie bald, wie schnell verrinnt die Zeit,
Ihr seid bei mir, ich bin bei Euch in Ewigkeit!

Süsses Herz Jesu sei meine Liebe!
300 Tage Ablass.
Süsses Herz Maria sei meine
Rettung! 300 Tage Ablass.

Another casualty of the British attacks on 8 May 1917 was twenty year old Anton Helsberger from Grünwald, who was killed by an artillery barrage at Chérisy, near Arras.

Zur frommen Erinnerung
im Gebete
an den ehr- und tugendsamen Jüngling
Johann Seidl,
Ökonomsohn von Linden,
Soldat beim bayer. Ref.=Fußart.=Regt. Nr. 3, 4. Batterie,
geboren den 24. Februar 1897, gestorben den Heldentod fürs Vaterland den 11. Mai 1917 am Hauptverbandsplatz der 6. Sanitätskompagnie infolge einer bei Arras erlittenen schweren Rückenverletzung durch eine Granate.

R. I. P.

O Eltern und Geschwister mein,
Ich kehre nicht mehr zu Euch heim,
Der letzte Gedanke, letzte Blick,
Der eilte noch zu Euch zurück.
Als ich starb im Feindesland,
Reichte niemand mir die Hand,
Doch eh' mein Auge war gebrochen,
Sah ich schon den Himmel offen.

Mein Jesus, Barmherzigkeit!

Vater unser.   Ave Maria.

J. & K. Mayr, Stadtamhof.

Johann Seidl, a twenty year old soldier in *4 Battery of 3 Bavarian Reserve Foot Artillery Regiment*, from Linden, died of wounds, caused by a shell, on 11 May 1917

Five decorated NCOs pose near Arras on Whit Sunday 1917.

Chapter Five

1918

Following a tour of the front and a series of staff conferences, on 21 January Ludendorff selected Operations Michael and Mars for the Spring offensive; preparations began immediately.

'After selecting the divisions and assembling the material available for the attack, it was decided to strike between Croiselles, south-east of Arras, and Moeuvres, and, omitting the Cambrai re-entrant, between Villers-Guislain and the Oise, south of St.Quentin.' Arras was not to be involved in the initial phase of the Kaiserschlacht.

Army territorial boundary changes saw the arrival of a new army on the front. *17 Army*, formerly *14 Army* in Italy, commanded by General von Below was put in between *2* and *6 Armies* opposite Arras. The boundary between *6* and *17 Armies* was half way between Arras and Lens, that between *2* and *17 Armies* was at Moeuvres. With *17 Army* making an attack on the line Croiselles-Moeuvres, this left a large section of the Arras front to be defended by *6 Army*. The possibility of

A view the British censor would never have allowed to be sent home.

With an attack pending on the western front the best troops from the eastern front were replaced by the worst from the west. Here officers pose on a train bound for the western front.

broadening the attack was anticipated and feints and preparations for further attacks were made between Ypres and Lens.

'By the day of the attack the British positions would be faced by over 3½ million soldiers, forming 194 divisions, of which sixty-seven were facing thirty-three enemy divisions. Secrecy was paramount. All important and large-scale troop movements should be carried out at night; no troop train could unload unless there were arrangements to disperse the men immediately. 'Safety Officers' controlled all means of communication and censored the mail. Any officer who knew any detail of the attack was sworn to secrecy. Secrecy was taken a stage further with the use of police aircraft and balloons to camouflage and search for any new tracks left by moving men and equipment. However, the possibility of an attack was deduced by the British from statements they took from deserters and their reconnaissance flights that showed the construction of large ammunition dumps and light railways.

The date of the attack was a well-kept secret until 18 March, when a German pilot who had been shot down revealed the date as either 20 or 21 March. When, on 19 March, this was corroborated by German prisoners and deserters, the only questions still in doubt on the British side were 'whether the first attack would be the main effort or merely a preparatory one, and whether or not the French would be attacked simultaneously.' So confident were the British that General Gough wrote home that night that he expected the bombardment would start on the night of 20 March, last between six and eight hours and be followed by German infantry on 21 March; he was only a few hours early with his prediction'.

'The assault troops were brought up to the front on 20 March without serious difficulty, even though the British artillery shelled the front line trenches during the evening and night. For the men in the first wave, time passed slowly, and tension rose as zero hour approached. Then, at the appointed time, 4.40 am on 21 March, nearly 10,000 field guns and mortars opened fire on the British positions on a front between the Oise and Sensée rivers, shelling the area between the forward positions and the battle zone; four hours later the first wave of infantry charged out of the trenches and moved quickly towards the British lines through thick fog. Preceded by the *Sturmabteilungen*, forty-three divisions of *Second* and *Eighteenth Armies* assaulted the British Fifth Army, while a further nineteen divisions of *Seventeenth Army* attacked the British Third Army. The well trained attackers were in excellent spirits and confident that they would win the war'.

'The infiltration tactics of the German infantry were eminently suited to the nature of the British defence, but were certainly favoured by the mistiness of the morning. The men of the advanced groups had rifles slung and made no attempt to use them, trusting to the stick bombs with which they were well provided. When they reached a trench they hurled their bombs and at once jumped in to settle the defenders with club or bayonet. The next parties pushed on through the gaps and then came others to deal with the centres of resistance by means of machine guns, flame projectors, trench mortars and field guns, and, in some instances, tanks. When the fog lifted the rearmost lines were exposed to view in masses, moving in column or forming up for attack, and these suffered heavily.'

Although the attack went well on the first day, it did not have the success hoped for and the advance was dealt with in the official daily communiqué in a brisk fashion: 'From south-east of Arras to La Fère we attacked the British positions. After a heavy bombardment of artillery and trench mortars our infantry assaulted on a wide front and everywhere captured the enemy's first lines.' Their success was of greater importance to the British commanders. For the attackers the only real advantage had been gained by *Eighteenth Army*, that had struck a weak spot. In general though, General von Kuhl, the Chief of the General Staff of the group containing the other two of the three attacking German Armies, stated that the hoped for objectives had not been reached, while his commander, Crown Prince Rupprecht, stated clearly 'that the expectation had been that the British artillery positions would be over-run', but this had not been fulfilled. There were also concerns about the serious losses of material in *Second* and *Seventeenth Armies* artillery units caused by British artillery fire.

The Bavarian Crown Prince concluded that the British Fifth Army was in the act of voluntarily retiring to the Crozat canal when the attack took place, and that on the front of *Second* and *Seventeenth Armies*, the British had planned to pull back to the 'Third Position' [the back line of the Battle Zone].

Only the Kaiser, who was in Supreme Command of the battle, and the German Crown Prince, believed that it was a victory; their feelings were not shared by any responsible commander and indeed Ludendorff made no remarks on the results of the first day. What is significant is that he left the heavy artillery with the attacking Armies which, 'if success were achieved, he had intended to shift northwards, in order to carry out the attack on Arras, so as to secure that pivot and lengthen the front of attack.'

Although the attacking forces continued to enjoy considerable success over the next few days, their progress did not come up to expectation. So on 25 March Ludendorff gave new instructions for the continuation of operations against the British by Crown Prince Rupprecht's group of Armies. 'First of all, the British front on both sides of the Scarpe as far as the Lens basin must be shaken and smashed by the attacks "Mars North" and "Mars South" and "Valkyrie", in combination. The attack would then be carried forward on both sides of Arras with the main pressure on the Lorette ridge towards Houdain. The attack between the La Bassée canal and Armentières should also be prepared, but in a reduced form'. St. George would become Georgette.

Tactically difficult and requiring thorough preparation, zero day for the Mars attacks was fixed as 28 March, with the date for the even more difficult attack against Lorette ridge being a day later. However, by 27 March the offensive was clearly showing signs of slowing down and the hopes that Mars would bring new life to the waning offensive power of *Second* and *Seventeenth Armies* were dashed. Aimed at the junction of two British armies, the attack only achieved slight gains of ground.

Facing the greater part of the attack were three high quality British divisions who were aware that an attack was imminent and whose commanders kept a minimum number of troops in the front line, in many cases relying on outposts rather than a line. The main line of defence was further back towards the rear of the forward zone of defence. Through the night the British troops were alert; the night was dark and the area eerily silent with the only activity in no man's land being British patrols.

King Ludwig of Bavaria at a march past of Bavarian troops on the Arras front in early 1918.

At 0300 hours the bombardment opened with mustard gas on British artillery positions. South of the Scarpe, from 0415 hours onwards, the bombardment was directed on the front trenches. An hour later the fire lifted, progressing from south to north. As the bombardment moved on, aircraft flew along the British lines, firing their machine guns as the infantry attempted to get through the British wire.

Although the bombardment had been accurate and effective, it had not destroyed the machine guns and trench mortars that were spread across the attack zone and housed underground until needed. As a result, the attacking troops, expecting little resistance, were met by every description of fire, and, although communication with their field guns was cut, the British artillery noted the changes in German artillery fire and followed suit. With such determined resistance the attacking troops were unable to make a general break-in and throughout the fighting heavy losses were sustained, as wave after wave came on through the smoke and shell-fire, forming excellent targets for the defenders.

Further north the attackers moved on with less difficulty, being hidden by the rolling ground near Monchy. Slowly but steadily the British troops moved back but the British Battle Zone still held, and by 1400 hours OHL was reporting to Second Army that Mars was a failure.

Aerial photo of the ground over which the 1918 Battle of Arras was to be fought, showing trench lines and destruction.

From 0840 hours a series of assaults was preceded by a barrage, allowing troops to infiltrate and turn the defence from the rear. In the face of such a determined attack the British troops slowly fell back during the afternoon, replacing losses with divisional cyclists and details from the wagon lines. However, as the result of over seven hours of heavy fire against them, the advance began to slacken with only isolated further attacks. By 1700 hours, Mars south had failed.

North of the Scarpe, seven divisions attacked two high quality British divisions preceded by a bombardment lasting four and a half hours, with the artillery being joined by trench mortars from 0500 hours. As a result most of the thinly held front line posts were obliterated. Nevertheless, when the attacking infantry advanced over the 100 yards No Man's Land, they were met with sufficient firepower to lose the advantage of their creeping barrage. However, progress was made in a swampy area between the two British divisions being attacked where the outposts had been destroyed by the German artillery, and at two other positions where the British defence was turned. In places the attackers were shoulder to shoulder and provided easy targets for the defending British troops, but sheer pressure of numbers pushed the defence back.

In order to boost troop numbers, the British divisions called up engineer companies and pioneer battalions but, even so, between 1000 and 1300 hours, further progress was made against the two British divisions. But, finding any advance over the open was too costly, the attackers, with artillery support, worked up the British communication trenches, cutting off some of the defenders. In some of the British sectors the situation was becoming critical; the order to retire was given to maintain contact with units on either side. To assist the attacking troops, field artillery batteries were sent forward, but these were caught and stopped by British shrapnel fire.

The British withdrawals consolidated the British line and enabled them to put up further resistance. This continuing resistance, combined with German losses, took the edge off the attack, and, although further attempts were made to force the line, they were not carried out with any great determination. To further assist the attackers, under the smoke of a heavy bombardment, field guns were brought forward, but these too were knocked out by British counter fire.

'At 4.15 and 5 p.m., infantry attacks were made on the 4th and 56th Divisions, respectively, both up the communication trenches and across the open; these were…repelled by the concentrated barrage of guns, machine guns and rifles.' Like its sister attack in the south, Mars North had also failed. By 1700 hours both attacks were at a standstill with heavy losses but even so Crown Prince Rupprecht's Army Group, convinced that victory was still possible between Albert and Arras, requested further divisions to resume the attack; OHL refused and the offensive was brought to a close. Although not the success that had been hoped for, the official communiqué that evening reported that 56 British Division had been annihilated!

On a military basis, a German writer poetically summed up the Mars attack: 'As the sun set behind rain clouds there also vanished the hopes which OHL had placed on the attack. "Mars", to whom so much blood was offered, was unable to break open the British Arras salient.' At midnight on 28 March, the Mars offensive was cancelled but the general attacks continued along the front with minor success. Apart from the determined resistance of the British defenders, a further factor was playing its part on the German side – hunger; only so much could be expected of troops who had been in action continuously for sixty-plus hours and had not eaten for forty-eight, except stocks available for plunder. There was a shortage of reinforcements so divisions had to be kept at the front to keep up the momentum. The troops were getting both physically and mentally tired. Some fought for eight days without taking off their boots or clothes, though this mattered less as the only water for washing was that in the shell holes. Even drinking water was in short supply. The offensive would now move north and Arras would again be a relatively quiet front for a few months.

'The offensives continued up and down the front with varying degrees of success until the Entente were able to launch their own offensive on 8 August at Amiens. At 4.20am on 8 August, Australian, British and Canadian troops, assisted by a devastating artillery bombardment, 800 aircraft and over 400 tanks, launched themselves at *Second Army*; by lunchtime the Entente success was virtually complete.'

'The official German account acknowledged that it was the greatest defeat since the start of the war with an estimated loss of up to 700 officers and 27,000 men, of whom about seventy per cent were POWs. And it was not only under-strength and tired divisions that failed to hold the enemy advance: at Hangard Wood, a fresh full strength division collapsed when attacked by Canadian troops. After the war the Germans blamed the defeat on the unprepared defensive position which looked pretty on the map, but in many cases merely amounted to a white tape on the ground to show where the line was supposed to be.'

'August 8th was the black day of the German Army in the history of this war', wrote General Ludendorff. 'This was the worst experience…except for the events that, from September 15th onwards, took place on the Bulgarian front and sealed the fate of the Quadruple Alliance.'

'However, the British attacks next day were not as successful and many of the senior commanders did not accept Ludendorff's black day scenario; by the next day it was clear that the men were recovering from the initial shock of the attack and that resistance was stiffening, with the effect that the British advance was slowing down. Fortunately neither the British or the French were able to exploit their tactical success and the position stabilised for the defenders.'

The British Official History agreed with senior German commanders and their appraisal of the first day of the offensive, 'on the face of it, the 8th August hardly seems to have deserved the fatal label of "the black day of the German Army".'

Casualties had been high but they were even higher for the attackers. The question of morale was once again visited when casualty rates were analysed: sixty-nine percent of the casualties were missing, the majority assumed to have become POWs.

After 15 August 'there were indications of an offensive between Arras and the Ancre, especially towards Bapaume. The *17th Army* was not to hold its front line but to give battle in a position three to four kilometres in rear; the front line was merely to be held by outposts who were to fall back on to the main position before the attack.'

Although the troops were withdrawing, many had not lost the will to fight, raiding enemy trenches and shelling the trenches overnight with gas to make them untenable for the British troops. However, much of the area around Arras was regarded as a quiet one. Indeed, the British 8 Division felt that the troops facing

A relatively quiet night at the front.

them north of Arras, were well sheltered in deep-dug trenches behind strong belts of wire, showing little inclination to fight unless pushed.

'On August 21st the English attacked south of Arras between Boisleux and the Ancre; this was the first of a series of attacks on Crown Prince Rupprecht's sector which lasted almost uninterruptedly to the end of the war and made the heaviest demands on the Group Headquarters and their armies.' Five days later, after *17 Army* had pulled back successfully, 'the English offensive against the Arras-Cambrai road opened.'

While some areas were evacuated, others fought on regardless. After Gavrelle was evacuated, British troops quickly occupied and started to move north only to be met with determined resistance from the defenders in Oppy who delivered four counter-attacks against British positions on 28 August. Then, just as quickly as it had flared up, the fighting died down.

The troops fell back according to plan but eventually further British attacks broke the Drocourt-Quéant line and reached the Wotan position. 'On September 2nd a strong assault by English tanks over-ran obstacles and trenches in this line and paved a way for their infantry.' As a result *17 Army* requested and were given permission to retire to a new line in front of the Arleux-Moeuvres Canal; during the night of 3 September it withdrew behind the canal; such withdrawals shortened the line and economised on manpower.

'OHL recognized defeat' and about mid-day 2 September 'issued orders for retirement behind the Sensée and the Canal du Nord' beginning that night. The movement was to pivot on the River Scarpe near Etaing, east of Arras, with a new

Out of the line men had the luxury of a hot meal provided straight from the cooker – a midday meal in enemy territory.

defensive line running eastwards along the north bank of the Sensée to near Arleux. By the morning of 3 September, *Seventeenth Army,* which held positions on the Arras front to near Lens, had occupied a new position from Havrincourt through Marquoin, Arleux and Sailly-en-Ostrevent. The next day raids took place against British posts around Oppy.

Crown Prince Rupprecht was returning to the front after sick leave on the day OHL issued its retirement orders. There was considerable unrest over the continuation of the war, as he recorded in his diary: 'In Nürnberg the inscription on a troop train was to be read: "Slaughter cattle for Wilhelm & Sons". Public feeling, for that matter, is not only very bad in Bavaria, but also in North Germany'.

At the OHL conference at Avesnes, on 6 September, Ludendorff blamed both leaders and troops for the events of the past few days. He also gave notice that as a result of troop shortages, infantry battalions would be reduced from four to three companies and baggage would be cut down to reduce transport needs. He then demanded sharp measures against shirkers. On the same day, British troops raided Oppy village in a tit-for-tat attack to be followed by an attack on British positions on 16 September with the inevitable retaliation the same night. There were further British raids on 20 and 26 September resulting in casualties on both sides for little or no real gain.

On 22 September, General von der Marwitz was removed from command of the *Seventeenth Army*, after the failure of a counter-attack by three nearly fresh divisions, near Havrincourt, at 1700 hours on 18 September.

South of Arras, on 27 September, the British Third Army started a new offensive. The same day, on the Arras front, the British 20 Division made a successful diversionary attack against the Fresnoy sector north of Oppy. While the main Allied thrust was to the south there was intermittent hostile shelling and ordinary harassing fire by British heavies, day and night, with field guns and machine guns joining in at night.

With continued pressure from Allied attacks, casualties mounted so severely, that, on 30 September, Hindenburg telegraphed the Army Groups with the information that they could no longer assume that OHL reserves would be available; nevertheless 'an enemy break-through must in all circumstances be prevented' and every effort must be made to gain time and inflict heavy losses on the enemy while the Hunding-Brunhild Stellung was prepared.

The manpower shortage is confirmed in regimental histories, with battalions being reported as being down to an average of 150 men. Those that were left were a shadow of the their former selves: 'the troops were completely used up and burnt to cinders'.

On 2 October, in the northern sector of British First Army front at Arras, Allied troops discovered that there was little or no opposition in front of them, except for the area around Cité St. Auguste. The next day troops from British VIII Corps found that Lens had been evacuated by *Sixth Army*. However, further south, resistance was stiffer though the British troops made progress, except in the most southern sector of British VIII Corps where there was no German retreat; the troops were firmly entrenched.

Well entrenched and capable of considerable resistance, but time and Allied pressure were against them. After confused fighting in a counter-attack which saw both sides fighting each other in both sets of trenches simultaneously, the final battle in the Oppy sector commenced on 6 October when British troops bombed their way along the trenches, cutting off Oppy from other defensive positions and capturing the garrison.

The fall of Oppy opened up the whole southern sector, and the next day Allied attacks pushed through the powerful defence line between Biache-St. Vaast and the

Fresnes-Gavrelle road to the north; by the evening the greater part of the system between Oppy and the Scarpe had been taken by the British 8 Division. The fighting showed that the defenders had no immediate intention of evacuating the area. However, determined British attacks pushed the defenders back and by 9 October the battle had moved on towards the Drocourt-Quéant line. There was a similar story all the way along the Arras front and on the British Third and Fourth Army fronts.

On 9 October, Izel fell to British troops and, after an unsuccessful counter-attack by the defenders, Rouvroy was found to have been evacuated. Two days later, 8 British Division attacked the Drocourt-Quéant positions to the north of the Gavrelle-Brebières road to find only rear-guard parties who informed the attackers that the division had left hours earlier. Similar attacks by British troops found the same situation – evacuated positions.

The next day the British First Army continued its advance on both flanks, with the left wing being hampered more by the waterlogged and – in places – flooded levels of the Douai plain, than by any resistance. British units found many positions unoccupied or being evacuated. There was only occasional resistance from the defenders, although in key villages like Arleux this could still considerable. Defending units did not always make things easy for the future occupiers, leaving behind presents to catch out the attacking troops: Corbehem and its suburbs 'were found to be full of mines and booby traps', so much so that they could not be occupied until engineers cleared the place.

In general, the further eastwards the attackers moved the greater the defence; an artillery bombardment was required on Douai prison and the outlying area before the defenders moved on. In some areas resistance from machine guns and field artillery was sufficient to stop the British advance and on 13 October a local counter-attack succeeded in pushing back the advancing British troops at Aubigny au Bac. Another means of holding the Allied attack was cutting the banks of the River Scarpe. By 16 October the front had stabilised in front of a canal line with only a few footings beyond it.

17 October brought further withdrawals with little opposition except from artillery, leaving the British troops with insufficient bridging material to follow. Those units that scrambled across the destroyed bridges or crossed by raft encountered little opposition, while Douai had been evacuated and left to burn. The war on the Arras front was over until next time – 1940.

Newly arrived troops learning how to set up and use a small trench mortar.

Heavy artillery carefully camouflaged and ready for the British attack.

One complaint along the front was the youth of the new replacements. Here two youthful soldiers pose for a last photo before leaving home for the front.

As Allied airpower grew, it became more necessary than before to camouflage everything.

The trench mortar soldiers were a law unto themselves. Positions were set up along the front, mortars fired and then they moved on, leaving the trench soldiers to receive the Allied retaliation.

A heavy trench mortar lends its weight to the artillery barrage against the British troops holding the positions around Arras in the Mars offensive.

Anton Müller, a farmer's son from Reichsdorf, holder of the Iron Cross Second Class and a reservist with *1 Company of 13 Infantry Regiment* who died a hero's death on 24 March 1918 in an artillery barrage at Boiry near Arras.

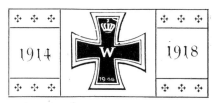

Andenken im Gebete

an den tugendsamen Jüngling

Anton Müller

Bauerssohn von Reichsdorf

Inhaber des Eisernen Kreuzes II. Cl.
Reservist beim 13. Inf.-Reg., 1. Komp.,

den Heldentod gestorben am 24. März 1918 durch Artillerieschuss vor BOIRY (bei Arras) im Alter von 29 Jahren. Er liegt bei seinen Kameraden begraben.

＞＜＞＜＞

Abschied von Deinen lieben Eltern
Nahmst Du auf Nimmerwiederseh'n,
Und uns, den Eltern und Geschwistern,
Wollt' ob dem Weh das Herz vergeh'n.
Schwer ist der Schlag der uns getroffen,
Zerrissen ist das schöne Band. —
Doch süsser Trost ist uns geblieben:
Du starbst als Held für's Vaterland!

C. SCHREIBAUER, EICHENDORF.

With a shortage of men and materials, equipment was likely to break or wear out.

A knight of the road –
drivers had their own
uniform and stood apart
from the normal soldier.

Out on rest – did every unit have one soldier who felt
the need to dress as a woman?

A heavily fortified dugout, complete with water butt.

A light field artillery piece, heavily camouflaged and ready.

Storm troopers were the cream of the army – here a section poses for the camera before moving to the front.

Field artillery laying down a barrage during the winter of 1917/1918.

Generalleutnant Ludendorff.

A sight to bring a smile to troops who were starved, literally, of food – a provision wagon on its way to the front.

The second enemy in the trenches: every army suffered from lice. Here soldiers are cleaned and their clothes fumigated – clean for a few minutes until they went back into the trenches.

The war over, 7 *Bavarian Field Artillery Regiment* arrive back in Munich on 22 November 1918.

Along with lice, rats were a constant problem. Dogs provided companionship and also liked to kill rats; here, Greÿ shows off his trophies.

Chronology of the Arras Front
1914-1918

1914

6 September. German cavalry enter Arras.

9 September. French light cavalry force German troops out.

30 September. French re-enter the city.

5 October. Bavarian troops force French XXI Corps from Souchez, Givenchy and Vimy Ridge to the north of Arras but French counter-attacks stabilize the line north and south of the city.

6 October. Arras heavily bombarded. French positions hold against heavy attacks.

10 October. Battle of La Bassée.

21 October. Shelling destroys Arras town hall's 16th century belfry tower.

1 November. French positions near Vimy attacked, using grenades for the first time.

7 November. Heavy fighting at Arras.

28 November. Attacks made on French positions around Arras.

12 December. Proposed offensive by French Tenth Army in the Arras and Vimy area is delayed until 17 December.

17 December. French attacks on a 1¼ mile front near Arras fail due to fog and inadequate artillery preparations. German defence results in nearly 8000 French casualties for minimal gain.

18 December. First German trench mortar units formed, with six light mortars per pioneer company.

26 December. Deep mud delays any possible French advance; French Tenth Army attack postponed as a result.

27 December. Ten battalions of French Chasseurs Alpins capture 800 yards of trenches at La Targette, from Bavarian troops after a two hour artillery preparation.

28 December. Non-stop rain halts all but small local operations.

Beaurains, a suburb of Arras, from the surrounding heights.

Safe behind the lines, wounded soldiers rest in the hospital garden in Croisilles.

Troops attending the burial of their company commander in the church cemetery at Douchy les Ayette.

Each village had a sentry to check papers and direct traffic; this soldier was guarding Hendecourt.

Watchtower built into a tree at Ficheux; on level terrain such positions were invaluable for the view they gave of French positions.

High ranking officers occupied the best accommodation in the area – the interior of the château at St. Léger after its requisition.

Like mail from home, religion played an important part in the soldiers life – a padre preaches to his congregation in a cave, safe from enemy shelling.

Prince Leopold of Bavaria, with the commander of *3 Bavarian Armeekorps* visits the troops at the front.

A squadron of Bavarian cavalry set out on patrol.

Keeping the front provisioned required thousands of horses, wagons and men: a provisions column moving to the front.

1915

3 January. Limited French gains near Arras.

15 January. Some trenches taken a month earlier by the French, on Notre Dame de Lorette ridge and at Carency, are re-taken.

16 January. Seesaw battle for St Laurent-Blangy, northeast of Arras; positions finally recaptured by the French.

28 January. French positions at Bellacourt, southwest of Arras, attacked, but with no major result.

4 February. French attack on positions at Ecurie, north of Arras, is successful, and front line is taken.

17 February. Minor French advance near Arras.

20 March. French trenches near Notre Dame de Lorette taken.

21 March. Newly taken positions near Notre Dame de Lorette lost to French counter-attack.

25 March. Control of Notre Dame Ridge lost to French, who repulse counter-attack.

16 April. French repulse attacks on Notre Dame de Lorette.

3 May. Preliminary French bombardment of positions around Arras commences with an offensive expected.

4 May. French bombardment around Arras intensifies, using 1073 guns and 92 mortars firing 690,000 shells.

7 May. French artillery concentrates on specific targets to the north of Arras but, without high-ground observation, are unsure of effect on German positions.

8 May. During the night, the French blow five mines as a prelude to the attack but lose their objective to successful counter-attack.

9 May. French launch the second battle of Artois after a final four hour bombardment from 1000 guns. French troops storm through up to 3^1/$_2$ miles on a four mile front, at Vimy ridge, in just 90 minutes. Successful counter-attack regains Souchez before the French can reinforce the position. French cut off Carency and storm La Targette. In just ten minutes' fighting to the northeast of Arras, the French X Corps sustains 3000 casualties.

11 May. Fort and chapel of Notre Dame de Lorette lost to French XXI Corps attack, but Lorette ridge heights held against French XXXIII Corps attacks. After considerable losses, Petain stops further French frontal attacks.

12 May. 1000 POWs lost when French take Carency.

20 May. 'White Road' near Souchez lost to French attack.

27 May. French capture positions at Les Quatre Bouquetaux and Ablains - St. Nazaire.

28 May. After savage hand-to-hand fighting, French take positions in 'The Labyrinth' north of Arras.

30 May. Some positions lost to French attacks near Souchez.

31 May. Souchez sugar refinery stormed by French troops.

1 June. After French attacks some positions around Souchez lost.

5 June. French attacks north of Arras and east of Lorette ridge successfully counter-attacked.

8 June. French troops make further progress in 'The Labyrinth'. All of Neuville-St. Vaast lost to French attack.

11 June. French advance 1100 yards on a 1^1/$_4$ mile front.

13 June. French attack at Souchez held.

Officers inspecting a trench somewhere on the Arras Front in March 1915.

An exercise march out of the line of fire to keep the troops fit.

16 June. Major twenty division French assault, but only a Moroccan Division reaches Vimy Ridge crest.

18 June. Although French call off Second Battle of Artois, heavy fighting continues. Twenty-five square miles lost to French attacks.

19 June. Troops pull back after French attack at Souchez.

20 June. Unsuccessful counter-attack against French positions north of Arras.

7 July. Troops recover trenches lost to French attack at Souchez, and French troops fall back south of Souchez.

12 July. French positions in 'The Labyrinth' counter-attacked.

14 July. Positions south of Souchez lost to French attack and held against counter-attacks.

1 August. French repulse attacks and then occupy trenches in sunken road between Ablain and Angres.

4 September. Considerable artillery fire around Arras.

29 September. Vimy crest briefly lost to French attack.

1 October. French attack on La Folie Heights on Vimy Ridge pushes troops back.

6 October. Minor skirmishes with French troops.

10 October. Minor French gains in Souchez Valley, Givenchy-en-Gohelle Wood and the La Folie area.

14 November. Unsuccessful attack on French positions in 'The Labyrinth'.

21 November. Artillery duels with French.

24 November. Fifty shells fired at Arras railway station.

27 November. Unsuccessful trench raid on French positions north of 'The Labyrinth' while the French capture a crater to the north of it.

3 December. Fighting with aerial torpedoes northwest of Hill 140 and artillery duels along the front.

5 December. A few incendiary shells fired at Arras.

9 December. Artillery duel in the Givenchy sector.

Officers parading outside the officers mess at Ayette for a visiting civilian dignitary.

Alarm bell in the village square at Boyelles.

The only civilians left in the war zone were old men, women and children; here a delivery wagon is watched by a small boy as it passes through Cagnicourt, southeast of Arras.

The French children soon got used to the occupiers; here they pose for the photographer in a field outside Croisilles.

Looking south down a street in Douchy les Ayette with directions painted on the buildings – Ayette to the east and Adinfer to the north.

Leutnant Immelmann posing in front of his Fokker aircraft on 26 October 1915, at Ecoust St. Martin airfield, after scoring his fifth victory.

Underground accommodation built into a quarry at Ficheux.

Hamélincourt - another church bell that was requisitioned to act as an alarm against air attack.

Soldiers were often buried where they fell, in the 1914 advance through the area - two lonely soldiers' graves near Henin-Cojeul.

Russian prisoners being guarded during a break in their work at St. Léger.

The back areas had to be kept safe – a police patrol leaving St. Léger.

Letters from home helped keep the soldier happy – the Field Post Office at St. Léger.

For those with the time and the resources, painting was a good way to pass the time. Here, an official War Artist poses for the camera before setting off to paint the battle.

To aid transport movement, walls were painted with directions. Ayette and Hamélincourt are signposted in the same direction, despite being in different directions to this north facing wall.

Rollencourt Château in December 1915 showing little damage.

The war was not always deadly. Here German and French soldiers are holding a conversation across the wire in what was termed the 'peaceful position war' during December 1915.

In December 1915, a soldier waits in an individual foxhole – in the background is Lorettohöhe.

Panorama of Givenchy-en-Gohelle showing the destruction of 1915.

Captured French trench mortar shells.

Street urchins selling goods in the street.

The town hall in Oppy became the battalion headquarters.

Oppy Château in quieter times when it was well behind the lines – November 1915.

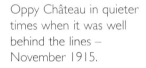

Oppy Wood was the site of a large cemetery in late 1915. By May 1917 when the war returned to it, there was no château and no cemetery.

Cooling the horses down in the Scarpe; horse transport was the main method of moving supplies and thousands of horses were used on the Arras front.

Column of French soldiers captured during the fighting between La Bassée and Arras in the autumn of 1915.

Allied prisoners taken during the autumn of 1915 – a mixture of English, French and Scottish troops.

Loading transport wagons on flat cars to speed the movement of supplies to the western front.

1916

22 January. Attack on French positions near Neuville-St. Vaast.

25 January. Attacks at Neuville renewed with mine explosions under French positions.

26 January. Further attacks on French positions at Neuville.

27 January. Attacks on French positions at Neuville continued.

8 February. 700 yards of French trenches taken west of La Folie.

10 February. Some of the newly taken trenches lost to a French counter-attack.

14 March. British troops complete take-over of Arras sector.

15 May. British mine and storm 250 yards of trenches on Vimy Ridge, but lose mine crater to counter-attack.

21 May. To counter British tunnelling at Vimy Ridge, after a fourteen hour barrage by 320 guns, *18 Reserve Infantry Division* captures 1500 yards of trench from 47 British Division; front line pushed 300 yards west into British positions.

23 May. A British two brigade counter-attack at Vimy is ruined by counter barrage that kills or wounds 2500 men.

31 August. British gas attacks on Arras front.

26 November. OHL issues instruction on role of forthcoming Siegfried Stellung: 'Just as in times of peace, we build fortresses, so we are now building rearward defences. Just as we have kept clear of our fortresses, so we shall keep at a distance from these rearward defences'.

18 December. General Marwitz takes over command of the *Second Army* from General Gallwitz.

After two years of occupation, much of the damage sustained in the opening months of the war had been repaired. Here troops cross a railway line on a replacement bridge.

With a shortage of male civilians, troops had to help the women gather in the harvest.

Memorial to the fallen soldiers of *164 Infantry Regiment,* from Hannover, in the churchyard at Boiry - Rictrude.

Russian prisoners of war in a work camp at Boiry-St. Martin.

Overseeing the making of a haystack at Croisilles.

Douai, at the northern end of the Arras front and well behind the lines, was an administrative and transportation centre. Troops not sent home for a period of leave were often sent here for a rest. This shows the town and the Scarpe canal.

Unloading lumber in a Pioneer park for conversion into timber for dugout construction.

Douchy-lès-Ayette was far enough behind the lines to be used to rest troops. It had to have its own cinema and football ground.

Garrison headquarters in Ecoust St. Martin, complete with sentry box (empty) and messenger on bicycle.

A carousel in Ficheux for soldiers to while away their time when resting between spells in the front line.

The interior of the officers' mess at Hamélincourt.

As often as was possible the dead were buried in official soldiers' cemeteries – this one is at Henin.

With food supplies always short, each division tried to supplement its food – a divisional pig pen at Inchy-en-Artois.

Life and death continued for the civilian population, even though the area was occupied – a funeral procession in St. Leger.

As the war progressed, telephone communication became more and more important. Here telephone engineers check the lines near St. Léger.

Communication trench at Monchy-au-Bois, southwest of Arras.

To counteract boredom, each area had a book depot where soldiers could borrow books – this one is at St. Léger.

Winter in the frontline trenches near Monchy-au-Bois.

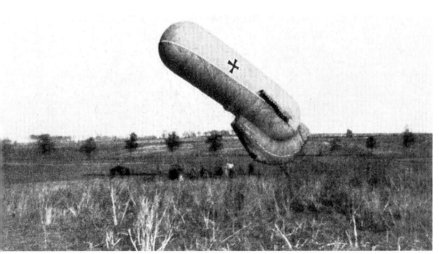

Observation balloons provided valuable information about what was happening on the other side of the wire – a divisional barrage balloon being launched at Moyenville.

A road block betweer Ransart and Berles au Bois in British territory.

Troops on the bridge over the river Souchez, down-stream from the local watermill. Note the single grave marker in the field behind the stream.

After six months of long range shelling, Rollencourt Château is reduced to a shell.

Leivin, May 1916, showing a regimental headquarters carefully hidden between two buildings.

The comfortable interior of the well-hidden regimental headquarters.

Hidden entrance to deep underground battalion headquarters in Leivin.

Weather conditions were very poor over the winter of 1915. This had been the front line trench in the old positions on the Giessler Heights in February 1916.

A battle trench on Giessler Heights in January 1916 showing a wooden drain to remove the water.

Kronprinzenlager storage area in Givenchy-en-Gohelle in April 1916.

The battalion defensive headquarters was also situated on Kronprinzlager.

A communication trench in the rear areas of Givenchy-en-Gohelle during February.

Communication trench in May 1916 on Vimy Ridge.

Both sides dug tunnels and laid mines under Vimy Ridge. Entrances were small to hide them from aircraft. When this photo was taken the tunnel was 20m deep under the enemy positions.

Soldiers were often buried near where they fell if conditions did not allow the removal of their body to a rear area cemetery. Here is a soldier's grave in a mine crater near the front line on Vimy Ridge.

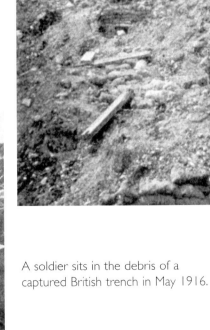

A soldier sits in the debris of a captured British trench in May 1916.

Hanseatenlager on Vimy Ridge, near Givenchy-en-Gohelle in May 1916. Areas like these provided shelter and storage.

This mine crater on Vimy Ridge, 50m wide and 20m deep, was caused by 180 hundredweight of explosive. Once it had been fought over and new trench lines consolidated, it provided ideal cover for a series of new mine tunnels.

The conditions on Vimy Ridge made it difficult to get the wounded away. Here soldiers make their way across the shell damaged hill with a wounded companion in a sling.

The front line on Vimy Ridge in February 1916.

Vimy Ridge seen from the 'White House' near Givenchy-en-Gohelle in June 1916.

Forward fighting trench on Vimy Ridge in March 1916. On the left is a trench periscope and a gasflag.

Taken in February 1916, a false gun battery. These were used to provide false information for reconnaissance aircraft and draw artillery fire away from real gun positions.

An open air concert in Sallaumines, outside the Regimental Commanders office, in May 1916.

Each village had a village commander (Ortskommandatur). These are the officers of the Ortskommandatur for Sallaumines in March 1916. They were known as the 'big star' and were situated on the road to Avion.

Sallaumines airfield with a crowd gathered to applaud the last combat victory of Oberleutnant Immelmann.

Before prisoners were taken to camps many of them were kept near the front to act as labourers. Here a group of prisoners mend the roads on the Arras front.

A heavy calibre British shell destroying the remains of a house on the Arras front.

Doaui town hall was turned into a regional headquarters, seen here complete with guard and sentry box.

House boats on the canal brought valuable supplies to the front.

Distributing food supplies to the local town's population.

A British aircraft that crashed at Cantaing. The pilot survived and is standing on the right in the long coat.

Small trench mortar in a concrete bunker.

Tunnellers digging 60 metres under the front line to lay explosives.

King Ludwig of Bavaria presenting medals to his soldiers during a visit to the Arras Front.

1917

1 January. Successful raid captures Hope Post from British.

16 January. British daylight trench raid west of Lens.

17 January. Daylight raid by the British on trenches west of Lens.

28 January. Crown Prince Rupprecht demands a voluntary retirement to the Siegfried Stellung as a result of the British pressure on the Ancre. Retirement vetoed by German OHL.

4 February. Operation Alberich authorised by the Kaiser: retirement to the Siegfried Stellung between Soissons in the south and Arras in the north; 65 miles long with average depth of 19 miles; whole area given the scorched earth treatment. Objective: release thirteen divisions into the reserve and shorten the front by twenty-five miles.

9 February. Operation Alberich begins on the Somme: demolitions and programmed removal of material and remaining civilian population.

12 February. Successful British trench raid south of Souchez.

13 February. Forty POWs lost to British trench raiders northeast of Arras.

22 February. Retirement to Siegfried Stellung accelerated due to British pressure, with a preliminary withdrawal of three miles on a fifteen mile frontage.

16 March. Synchronised retreat to Siegfried Stellung begun by thirty-five divisions.

20 March. British begin preparatory barrage for April offensive at Arras.

2 April. Further British pressure between Arras and St. Quentin results in the loss of nine villages, 700 killed and 240 POWs captured by the attacking troops.

4 April. British 2000 gun artillery barrage of gas and high explosive along twelve-mile front at Arras.

9 April. At 0530 hours, in bitter cold and sleet, the British attack on a twelve-mile front at Arras, breaching the third line defences, capturing 5600 POWs and thirty-six guns, in an advance varying from 2000 to 6000 yards. After a three minute barrage by 1203 guns and 150 Vickers machine guns, 30000 men of the Canadian Corps attack on a two mile front; five villages lost along with 4000 POWs and fifty-four guns, but the north end of Vimy Ridge is held against all Canadian attempts to capture it.

Machine gun position south of Arras.

With an officer overseeing the harvest work, soldiers and French women work together.

Every army has its pets – sometimes brought from home, and sometimes animals that attach themselves. For the garrison at Douchy-les-Ayette, Tell was a true companion.

Frontline trenches at Monchy-au-Bois; concrete is starting to replace the normal wood construction of the dugouts.

British tank knocked out during the Bullecourt battle.

10 April. Vimy Ridge lost when Hill 145 lost to Canadian attack after heavy fighting. The arrival of reserves starts to seal the gap in the Arras front.

11 April. Monchy-le-Preux and Wancourt lost to a British tank and infantry attack, but Allied infantry and tanks repulsed at Bullecourt, taking 1170 Allied POWs and capturing two tanks.

12 April. Pimple Hill stormed by Canadian infantry, but the Mericourt-Arleux line now held against an Allied breakthrough by two counter-attack divisions.

13 April. Villages of Vimy and Petit Vimy lost to Canadian attack. Heavy fighting at Wancourt Ridge, but line held against British attacks until 15 April.

14 April. Ten British soldiers hold Monchy-le-Preux against attacks from *3 Bavarian Division* for five hours. Canadian attacks result in loss of over 4000 POWs, 124 machine guns, 104 mortars and 54 field guns.

15 April. Four-division attack on a seven-mile front at Lagnicourt is checked by the Anzac Corps and 62nd Division.

22 April. General Falkenhausen replaced by General Below as commander of *Sixth Army*.

23 April. Troops pushed back after a British nine division assault on a nine-mile front across the River Scarpe preceded by artillery fire from 2685 guns. Of the twenty tanks used in the attack, five are disabled. Guémappe lost, five counter-attacks fail to take Gavrelle and 2500 POWs lost to the British. Heavy casualties inflicted on the attacking British troops.

28 April. Village of Arleux taken by Canadian attack along with 450 POWs, but further south, at Oppy, three British divisions held, inflicting heavy casualties, including 475 British POWs.

29 April. Some trenches lost to British attacks between Oppy and Gavrelle.

1 May. Losses fighting the British at Arras since 9 April include over 18000 POWs, over 450 guns and mortars, 470 machine guns and a territorial loss on a twenty mile front of between two and five miles in depth, against British losses of just under 84000 casualties.

3 May. Fourteen British divisions attack east of Arras on a sixteen mile front backed by 2685 field guns and 16 tanks. Attacking troops gain very little ground, although Fresnoy captured by the Canadians. Further south, six Australian and British divisions, assisted by twelve tanks, break through the Siegfried Stellung at Quéant.

6 May. Counter-attack near River Souchez repulsed by British.

7 May. Troops pull back between Bullecourt and Quéant as a result of Australian attack.

8 May. On the second attack, *5 Bavarian Division*, supported by 176 guns, recaptures Fresnoy near Arras.

11 May. Despite repeated counter-attacks by *80 (Reserve) Division*, Canadian troops hold 300 yards of trenches west of Avion. Cavalry Farm, Chemical Works and Roeux captured by the British.

12 May. Most of Bullecourt falls to British attack.

13 May. British push forward on Greenland Hill.

14 May. North of Gavrelle, troops pushed back by British attack.

15 May. Heavy fighting against the British around Bullecourt.

16 May. Counter-attacks against the British at Gavrelle fail. The Battle of Arras results in the loss of sixty-one square miles of territory, nearly 21000 POWs and over 250 guns in thirty-eight days of combat.

17 May. Bullecourt lost to British.

19 May. British attack positions to the northeast of Bullecourt.

20 May. First line of the Siegfried Stellung north of Bullecourt lost to British 33 Division.

21 May. Troops pull back against British attacks at Fontaine-les-Croisilles; British now hold advanced line of the Siegfried Stellung from Bullecourt to one mile east of Arras.

22 May. A day of infantry skirmishes and artillery duels.

Reserve troops waiting at a troop lager for the trucks to take them to the front to counter the British attacks during May.

Loading the trucks with men prior to going to the front.

26 May. First American troops disembark in France.

1 June. Ten divisions transferred from the Lens-Lille sector to Flanders.

3 June. After a 600-projector gas barrage, Canadian troops assault but cannot hold La Coulette south of the Souchez River; 100 POWs lost to attacking forces.

5 June. Some positions lost on Greenland Hill due to British attack.

8 June. A very strong raid by six Canadian battalions, west of Avion, takes more than 150 POWs and inflicts over 830 casualties after bombing over 150 dugouts.

14 June. Australian troops push defenders back on Infantry Hill.

15 June. Troops fail to hold Australian attack near Bullecourt.

18 June. Australians pushed back at Infantry Hill.

20 June. Attacks on the River Souchez and Infantry Hill repulsed by British and Australian troops respectively.

24 June. British night attack results in retreat from River Souchez positions.

26 June. British occupy La Coulotte, and Canadian Corps begins capture of Avion.

28 June. Heavy fighting results in the loss of Hill 65, a two mile stretch south of the River Souchez, most of Avion and an edge of Oppy Wood.

1 July. British attack on Liévin held.

14 July. Shelling of British positions southwest of Arras makes Lt. Genella the first American casualty (wounded by shell splinter).

16 July. Canadian troops relieve British opposite Lens and Hill 70.

23 July. *36 (Reserve) Division* loses 53 POWs during Canadian trench raid west of Lens.

2 August. Some British trenches stormed and held on Infantry Hill near Monchy-le-Preux.

3 August. Gains on Infantry Hill from 2 August lost. Allied attacks on the Scarpe successfully held.

Bavarian troops loaded up and ready to depart for the front in May 1917.

Reserves came from many different sources and distances. Here a troop convoy makes its way through dusty back roads heading for the Arras Front.

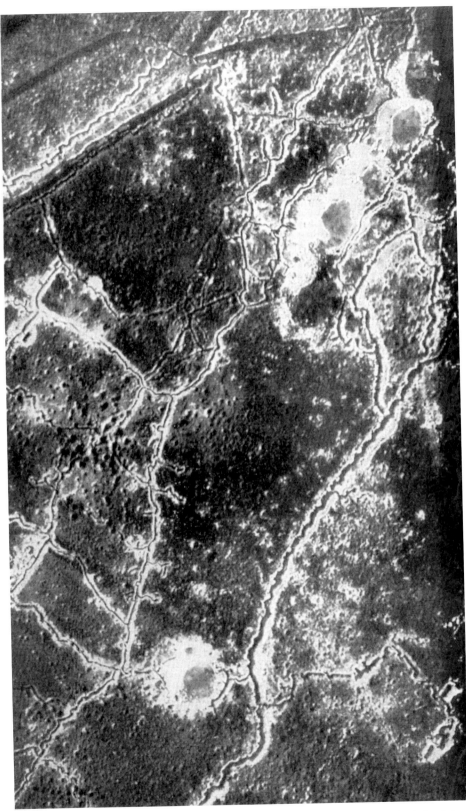

Aerial photo of Vimy Ridge; German positions on the right, Allied on the left of the mine craters. Note the saps pushed out from both trench lines to the rim of each mine crater.

15 August. Hill 70 north of Lens, and five nearby villages, lost to Canadian attack, supported by over 300 guns and 160 machine guns, even after over twenty counter-attacks (five divisions badly mauled by Canadian defenders); heavy casualties on both sides with nearly 1200 POWs taken by the attackers.

21 August. Near Lens, small amount of territory lost to a Canadian attack.

30 August. Light raid on British trenches southeast of Lens repulsed.

3 September. Four unsuccessful raids against British positions near Arleux.

29 September. First tank unit formed with 5 A7Vs and 113 men.

8 November. British troops succeed in raiding trenches near Fresnoy.

8 December. Over two hundred trench raids against British positions between this day and 21 March 1918, resulting in sixty-two enemy units being identified.

16 December. Troops retire under pressure from British forces east of Avion.

17 December. Fighting near the Ypres-Comines Canal.

After the Allied attack it was necessary for rear areas to be more prepared and ready for any future attack. Here a Cheval de Frise is by the roadside, between Lens and Henin Liétard, ready to be placed in the road to slow down troops and horses.

By May 1917 the headquarters of the Ortskommandatur for Sallaumines was a ruin.

Transferring supplies, well behind the front, directly from where they have been dropped off, for use in construction of fortified position in an embankment.

A street barricade at Izel, a few kilometres behind Gavrelle and Oppy which were attacked in April and May 1917.

Most transport was drawn by horses. Here at a cross-roads near Quiérry-la-Motte, troops drop off timber for use in trench construction during May 1917.

Field artillery using a damaged house as cover during the British attacks in May 1917.

An artillery unit forming up somewhere behind the Arras front in May 1917.

Field gun moving
up to its position
on the Arras front.

The rest barracks lay empty in May 1917 as all possible reserves
been committed to the front.

On the flatter parts of the front any
height advantage was seized upon to
give information about enemy
movements. Here a tree has been
turned into a watchtower.

The street from Monchy-le-Preux to Guémappe in April 1917 before the British attacked.

Town Hall on the right and entrance to the château at Monchy-le-Preux.

The regimental headquarters were in an ordinary house on the road to Roeux in April 1917.

The town square at Monchy-le-Preux in April 1917.

Any slight hill offered some protection. Here the face of a quarry near Roeux is being used as a protected area.

Plouvain in April 1917 – using the railway embankment as temporary housing.

The market square at Hamblain-les Prés in April 1917.

British aircraft losses were high during 'Bloody April'. The last flight of A2879 ended in Bois du Sart as the 15th victory of air ace Frankls.

Carrying hot meals to the front line from the rear areas was an arduous and sometimes dangerous job. Here ration carriers stop for a rest before crossing the Scarpe near Biache St. Vaast in May 1917.

Dressing station on the banks of the River Scarpe in May 1917.

Corbehem. On the junction of the Scarpe and Sensée canals this was an important town on the river transport system in June 1917.

Only a few kilometres behind the lines, little had changed. But this quiet street corner in Noyelle-sous-Bellone in May 1917 clearly shows directions to speed troop movements.

English POWs being escorted to the rear on their journey to a prison camp.

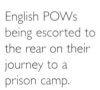

A garden in the centre of Doaui reserved for soldiers on leave, in June 1917.

Although leave was often cancelled when conditions dictated, here troops line up at a railway halt to wait for the train to take them to 'der heimat' in April 1917.

When no other accommodation was available, troops relied upon their waterproof capes to make a communal tent – zeltlager in May 1917.

Before the offensive, Bullecourt was a quiet village on the Arras front – the main street through the village.

The return train to the Hindenburg line in March 1917.

Trench positions ran deep on most of the front. Here, in the comparative quiet of a reserve trench in May 1917, soldiers take a rest.

Advanced dressing post in Cagnicourt during May 1917.

Ambulances arriving to take the wounded from the advanced dressing post at Cagnicourt.

A pioneer park in the rear echelons of the Arras front in May 1917. Essential supplies were stored there, ready for rapid transport using a small gauge railway.

Rest barracks in a stone quarry near Dury in May 1917.

Wagons parked in the main street of Arleux during June 1917, just behind the front areas near Oppy.

Erecting a hanger on an airfield.

A captured British plane painted with the Balkan Cross for use against its former owners in May 1917.

British aircraft N6186 at Cantaing in May 1917.

In the back areas life continued as per normal – a military concert in the Château park at Noyelles during May 1917.

Canadian soldiers in the trenches near Arras.

1918

3 January. Troops south of Lens pull back under pressure from British attacks.

9 January. Canadians raid positions south of Lens.

12 January. Four trench raids on British positions south of Lens and east of Monchy fail.

14 January. British raid positions north of Lens.

21 January. Spring offensive decision taken.

1 February. *Seventeenth Army* formed in Artois region. Captain Bomschlegel restores thirty captured British tanks ready for combat use.

12 February. Trenches near Hagnicourt-Lens raided by Canadian forces.

28 February. Western Front strength now 180 divisions due to arrival of troops from Russia.

1 March. Final preparations begin with advance parties moving up.

4 March. West of Lens, a raid on Aloof Trench, held by Canadian troops, fails.

5 March. New highly secure five-letter cipher introduced prior to offensive.

9 March. British front line, from Ypres to St. Quentin, bombarded with 1000 tons of Mustard and Phosgene gas.

10 March. Operation Michael ordered by Hindenburg.

20 March. 190 divisions now available on the Western Front.

March. Operation Michael commences. In the Artois region, British fire fifty-seven tons of Phosgene shells on positions near Lens.

26 March. Operation Mars launched with nine divisions against four divisions of British.

2 April. Ayette lost to British troops.

7 April. Attacks on British positions at Bucquoy repulsed.

21 May. Trenches near Arras raided.

8 June. Raid on Canadian trenches near Neuville-Vitasse repelled by Lewis gunner.

14 June. Trenches along La Bassée Canal raided by British troops.

22 June. Enemy tanks and infantry raid trenches at Bucquoy.

31 July. 1919 class of recruits almost used up as reinforcements.

1 August. Six British Infantry and two cavalry divisions leave the Arras area.

11 August. Ludendorff offers his resignation to the Kaiser who refuses it, and tells him that Germany has nearly reached the peak of its ability to resist and that 'the war must be ended'.

26 August. Canadian attack south of Arras, using tanks, captures Monchy-le-Preux and advances four miles.

27 August. Greenland Hill lost to British attack.

28 August. In the Artois region, troops have been pushed back up to five miles along the Arras-Cambrai road with the loss of 3300 POWs, fifty-three guns and 519 machine guns, but 2 Bavarian Corps hold on to the Fresnes-Rouvroy line.

29 August. Two villages lost to Canadian attacks along the Sensee river.

30 August. Hendecourt, behind the Fresnes-Rouvroy line, is lost to a British attack.

2 September. Drocourt-Quéant switch line, in the Wotan sector of the Siegfried Stellung, broken by enemy attack aided by tanks with the loss of 10000 POWs; Ludendorff issues order for a second phased retirement to the main defences behind and along the Canal du Nord.

3 September. Rapid retirement around Lens and enemy re-enter the town; 6000 POWs lost to advancing Canadians.

4 September. Unsuccessful raids on British positions in Arleux.

16 September. Successful raid on British positions near Oppy.

26 September. British attack on Oppy Wood held.

27 September. British offensive south of Arras.

29 September. Kaiser approves Hindenburg's and Ludendorff's request for an armistice.

1 October. Lens and Armentières evacuated during the night. Ludendorff sends a cable to Berlin government to transmit a peace offer without further delay.

5 October. Doaui is burned to make it useless to the enemy.

7 October. Gavrelle defences fail to hold British advance and, by the end of the day, Oppy falls.

8 October. Enemy attack on a twenty-mile front between St. Quentin and Cambrai takes the Fresnoy-Rouvroy line northeast of Arras.

11 October. Canadian troops capture Iwuy, northeast of Cambrai.

12 October. Deliberate flooding on 5 October halts British advance into Douai. Hindenburg warns the troops that continued resistance is necessary to obtain favourable armistice terms.

16 October. *Sixth* and *Seventeenth Armies* ordered to retreat into the Hermann Line.

19 October. Troops are pushed back nearly seven miles in a day and Denain is lost to advancing Canadians.

POST WAR

L. P. 3 - LA MAISON BLANCHE - (Environs d'Àrras) Cimetière Allemand 39.000 tombes - Military German Cemetery

At the end of the war the only German soldiers still on the Arras front were in cemeteries like Maison Blanche where there were 39000 burials.

During the Great War French railways carried men in wagons designed for either 15 horses or 40 men. In 1940 they were again used for 40 men – nationality unspecified.

In 1940 the guards again arrived to protect each village just as in the First World War.

Most of the cemetery memorials were destroyed after the war. This one at Fresnes survived and is now part of a farmer's yard.

Bibliography

Barrie, A. *War Underground*. Tom Donovan Publishing, 1961

Becke, Major A.F. *Military Operations France & Belgium, 1918 volume 1*. Macmillan & Co, 1935

Behrmann, F & Brandt, W. *Die Osterschlacht bei Arras 1917*. Stalling, 1929

Bilton, D. *Oppy Wood*. Pen & Sword Books Ltd, 2005

Brown, M. *1918 Year of Victory*. Sidgwick & Jackson, 1998

Chickering, R. *Imperial Germany and the Great War, 1914-1918*. Cambridge University Press, 2005

Doyle, A.C. *The British Campaign in France and Flanders 1916*. Hodder and Stoughton, 1918

Duffy, C. *Through German Eyes: the British and the Somme 1916*. Weidenfeld & Nicholson, 2006

Edmonds, Brigadier General Sir James, CB, CMG. *Military Operations France & Belgium 1914*. Macmillan & Co, 1922

Edmonds, Brigadier General Sir James, CB, CMG. *Military Operations France & Belgium 1915*. Macmillan & Co, 1928

Edmonds, Brigadier General Sir James, CB, CMG. *Military Operations France & Belgium 1916*. Macmillan & Co, 1932

Edmonds, Brigadier General Sir James, CB, CMG. *Military Operations France & Belgium 1917*, volume 2 Messines and 3rd Ypres. HMSO, 1948

Edmonds, Brigadier General Sir James, CB, CMG. *Military Operations France & Belgium 1918*, volume 2. Macmillan & Co, 1937

Edmonds, Brigadier General Sir James, CB, CMG. *Military Operations France & Belgium 1918*, volume 3. Macmillan & Co, 1939

Edmonds, Brigadier General Sir James, CB, CMG. *Military Operations France & Belgium 1918*, volume 4. HMSO, 1947

Edmonds, Brigadier General Sir James, CB, CMG. *Military Operations France & Belgium 1918*, volume 5. HMSO, 1947

Falls, Captain C. *Military Operations France & Belgium 1917. The German retreat to the Hindenburg Line and the Battle of Arras*. Macmillan, 1940

Foley, R. *German Strategy and the Path to Verdun*. Cambridge University Press, 2005

Görlitz, W (ed). *The Kaiser and his Court* (the First World War diaries of Admiral Georg von Müller). Macdonald. 1961

Gray, R & Argyle, C. *Chronicle of the First World War Volume 1, 1914–1916*. Facts on File, 1991

Gray, R & Argyle, C. *Chronicle of the First World War Volume 2, 1917–1921*. Facts on File, 1991

Hahn, Dr. *Zwischen Arras und Peronne*. R Piper & Co. Verlag, 1916

Hedin, S. *With the German Armies in the West*. John Lane, 1915

Hull, I. *Absolute Destruction*. Cornell University Press, 2005

Johnson, J.H. *Stalemate!* Arms & Armour Press, 1997

Junger, E. *Storm of Steel*. Chatto & Windus, 1929

Keegan, J. *Passchendaele, Volume 6, History of the First World War*. Purnell, 1971

Kitchen, M. *The German Offensives of 1918*. Tempus, 2005

Ludendorff, General. *My War Memories 1914-1918 volume 2*. Hutchinson (no date)

Mason, D. *The Aisne. Volume 1, History of the First World War*. Purnell, 1969

Miles, Captain W. *Military Operations France & Belgium 1917. The Battle of Cambrai*. HMSO, 1949

Nicholls, J. *Cheerful Sacrifice*. Leo Cooper, 1990

Ousby, I. *The Road to Verdun*. Jonathan Cape, 2002

Passingham, I. *All the Kaiser's Men*. Sutton Publishing, 2003

Passingham, I. *Pillars of Fire*. Sutton Publishing, 1998

Poseck, M von. *The German Cavalry*. E S Mittler & Son, 1923

Sheldon, J. *The German Army on the Somme 1914 – 1916*. Pen & Sword, 2005

The Times. Documentary History of the War. Volume 5. The Times Publishing Company, 1918

Thomas, N. *The German Army in World War I (3) 1917 – 18*. Osprey, 2004

Thorold, B. *Invasion. Volume 1, History of the First World War*. Purnell, 1969

Unknown authors. *Die Schlacht bei Arras*. R Piper & Co. Verlag, 1918

Various authors. *Canada in the Great World War*. United Publishers of Canada, 1920

Westman, S. *Surgeon with the Kaiser's Army*. William Kimber, 1968

Williams, J. *The Home Fronts 1914 – 1918*. Constable, 1972

Wood, H.F. *Vimy!* Macdonald, 1967

Young, Brigadier P. *The Great Retreat. Volume 1, History of the First World War*. Purnell, 1969